COMPREHENSION: GRADE 4
TABLE OF CONTENTS

INTRODUCTION

This book is designed to help students become better readers. The IRA/NCTE Standards for the English Language Arts lists as their first recommendation: "Students read a wide range of print and nonprint texts to build an understanding of texts, of themselves, and of the cultures of the United States and the world; to acquire new information; to respond to the needs and demands of society and the workplace; and for personal fulfillment. Among these texts are fiction and nonfiction, classic and contemporary works." A variety of reading selections attract and hold the interest of students. The activities in this book contain high-interest reading selections that cover a wide range of subjects in such areas as science, social studies, history, sports, and the arts.

ORGANIZATION

Each of the six units focuses on essential reading comprehension skills: finding the facts, detecting a sequence, learning new vocabulary through context, identifying the main idea, drawing conclusions, and making inferences.

- **FACTS:** Literal comprehension is a foundation skill for understanding a reading selection. Students using the Facts unit practice identifying pieces of factual information presented in each reading selection. The focus is on specific details that tell who, what, when, where, and how.

- **SEQUENCE:** Sequence involves the time order of events and the temporal relationship of one event or step to other events or steps. Reading for sequence means identifying the order of events in a story or the steps in a process.

- **CONTEXT:** When students practice using context, they must use all the words in a reading selection to understand the unfamiliar words. As they develop this skill, students become aware of the relationships between words, phrases, and sentences. The skill provides them with a tool that helps them understand words and concepts by learning how language is used to express meaning. Mastering this skill allows students to become independent readers.

- **MAIN IDEA:** When students read for the main idea, they must read to recognize the overall point made in the reading selection. Students must be able to differentiate the details from the main idea. They must understand the one idea that is supported by all the details in the selection. Identifying the main idea involves recognizing or making a generalization about a group of specifics.

- **CONCLUSION:** Drawing a conclusion is a complex reading skill because a conclusion is not stated in a reading selection. Students are asked to draw a conclusion based only on the information within a selection. They must put together the details from the information as if they were clues to a puzzle. The conclusion they draw must be supported by the details in the reading selection.

- **INFERENCE:** Students make inferences by combining their own knowledge and experiences with what they read. They must consider all the facts in the reading selection. Then they must put together those facts and what they already know to make a reasonable inference about something that is not stated in the selection. Making an inference requires students to go beyond the information in the text.

USE

The activities in this book are designed for independent use by students who have had instruction in the specific skills covered in the lessons. Copies of the activity sheets can be given to individuals or pairs of students for completion. When students are familiar with the content of the worksheets, they can be assigned as homework.

To begin, determine the implementation that fits your students' needs and your classroom structure. The following plan suggests a format for this implementation.

1. **Administer** the Assessment Test to establish baseline information on each student. This test may also be used as a post-test when the student has completed a unit.

2. **Explain** the purpose of the worksheets to the class.

3. **Review** the mechanics of how you want students to work with the activities. Do you want them to work in pairs? Are the activities for homework?

4. **Introduce** students to the process and purpose of the activities. Work with students when they have difficulty. Give them only a few pages at a time to avoid pressure.

5. **Do** a practice activity together. Review with students how to do each comprehension skill by using the practice example provided in the Overviews.

OVERVIEW: FACTS

Introducing the Skill

Remind students that facts are things they can taste, touch, feel, smell, and see. Explain that successful readers pay close attention to details. Emphasize that the questions in the Facts unit ask about details stated in the reading selections. Students should be able to show where the answer to a question is located in a selection.

How the Lessons Are Organized

A lesson consists of a reading selection about a single topic broken into two parts. Each part is followed by four questions that require students to find the facts in the selection.

Practice Activity

Read this story to your students.

Coober Pedy

Opals are stones that sparkle with many colors. Some of the most beautiful opals come from a town in South Australia. This town is called Coober Pedy. Opals were first found there in 1915. Tourists like to visit this town. They come to buy opals and to see the unusual buildings. Coober Pedy gets very hot in the summer. So most people build their homes underground. In this way the homes stay cool in the summer and warm in the winter. Tourists can stay in an underground hotel.

Have students answer the following questions about the story.

1. When were opals first found at Coober Pedy?
   A. in 1991   C. in summer
   B. in 1915   D. in winter

2. Tourists like to visit Coober Pedy
   A. to swim   C. to buy opals
   B. to dig   D. to learn to cook

3. Coober Pedy gets hot in the
   A. summer   C. spring
   B. fall   D. winter

4. Where can tourists stay?
   A. in a camp   C. in an apartment
   B. in a house   D. in an underground hotel

Explain to students that they should look for facts while reading the stories. They should read each question carefully and try to find a sentence in the story that has some of the same words as the question.

OVERVIEW: SEQUENCE

Introducing the Skill

Remind students that when they read, the events or steps presented in a story have a special sequence. Explain that clue words, like *today, then, first, after, then, finally,* can help them find what happens first, next, and last in a story. Tell students that sequence can also be implied. Finding sequence without signal words means paying careful attention to verb tense. Another clue to implied sequence is the order in which information is presented. Students need to know that writers usually try to relate the events in a story in order. If there are no time signals, students can assume that events have occurred in the order in which they are presented.

How the Lessons Are Organized

A lesson consists of a reading selection about a single topic, followed by five questions. The first question asks students to put statements in order based on the information in each selection. The following questions ask about the stated or implied sequence in each selection.

Practice Activity

Read this story to your students.

The Crane

Long ago a woodcutter and his wife lived in the forest. One day he found a lovely, white crane caught in a hunter's trap. He freed the crane and went back to work. That night, a young girl knocked on the couple's door. They took her inside. The next day, she gave them a beautiful piece of woven cloth and told them to sell it for a high price. Each day she gave them a new piece of cloth. On the seventh night, the woodcutter woke up. He saw a crane sitting at the loom weaving cloth from its feathers. The crane said, "I am here to repay you for saving me. But now I must go." It said good-bye and then flew away.

Have students answer the following questions about the story.

1. Put these events in the order that they happened. What happened first, second, last?
   A young girl knocked on the couple's door. (2)
   The woodcutter freed the crane from a trap. (1)
   The girl gave the couple beautiful cloth. (3)

2. When did the woodcutter see the crane at the loom?
   A. that evening
   B. at noon on the second day
   <u>C. on the seventh night</u>

3. What happened just before the crane flew away?
   A. The crane gave a cry of pain.
   <u>B. The crane said good-bye.</u>
   C. The crane wove cloth from its feathers.

Explain to students that they should find words in the questions that are the same as words in the story, find time words in the story, and look at the order of the events in the story.

OVERVIEW: CONTEXT

Introducing the Skill

Review this skill with students by using a simple cloze-type procedure. Ask students to supply the missing word in "The pretty, yellow ___ swam happily in the pond." Discuss how they know the word is *fish*. Remind students to pay attention to the meaning of surrounding words and phrases. Also, have them focus on language clues such as the position of the unknown or missing word in the sentence and what kind of words come before and after it.

How the Lessons Are Organized

A lesson consists of four reading selections. In lessons 1 through 6, the selections are presented in a cloze format with one or two missing words. In lessons 7 through 12, the selections contain a word in boldface type. Students are asked to use the context of the selection to choose the correct definition for each boldfaced word.

Practice Activity

Read these stories to your students. Have them choose the word that completes each sentence.

Animals have different kinds of feet. Squirrels have long toes with sharp _(1)_ that help them climb trees. A mountain goat's _(2)_ help it go up steep cliffs.

1. A. fingers   <u>B. claws</u>   C. gloves   D. knives
2. <u>A. hooves</u>   B. hands   C. nails   D. boots

Eskimos use **kayaks** to travel the icy waters where they live. Kayaks are like canoes, but they have room for only one person.

3. In this paragraph, the word **kayaks** means
   A. sleds   <u>C. boats</u>
   B. skis   D. planes

Remind students that to use context, they should keep reading even if they find a word they do not know. The right answer is the word that goes with the other words in the story. If they can't find the answer the first time, they should look back at the story.

OVERVIEW: MAIN IDEA

Introducing the Skill

Have students recall a movie that they have recently seen. Ask them to state the plot of the movie using one sentence. Explain that this sentence is the main idea of the movie. Point out the difference between the main idea of the movie and the details that support the main idea. Stress that all of the details add up to the main idea.

How the Lessons Are Organized

A lesson consists of three or four short reading selections for which students are asked to identify the main idea. Lessons 1 through 6 have stated main ideas, while lessons 7 through 12 have implied main ideas.

Practice Activity

Read this story to your students.

There are more than three thousand kinds of frogs. The grass frog is so small it can sit on an acorn. The goliath frog of West Africa is the largest frog in the world. It is the size of a cat. The water-holding frog uses the skin it has shed to make a bag around itself. This bag holds in water and keeps the frog cool.

The story mainly tells
A. about the goliath frog
B. about a tiny frog
C. that there are many kinds of frogs
D. about the water-holding frog

For Lessons 1-6, have students read the whole story. Then they should ask themselves, "Which sentence is the sum of all the other sentences?" Explain that the main idea will be that sentence.

For Lessons 7-12, have students read the whole story. Then they should figure out what the details have in common. Tell them to think about what the writer is trying to tell them.

OVERVIEW: CONCLUSION

Introducing the Skill

Emphasize that practicing this skill means thinking about what is actually stated in the reading selection. Ask students what they can conclude from the sentence, "Sylvia rushed into the kitchen and yanked the cookies from the smoking oven." Students can conclude that Sylvia was not in the kitchen before she pulled the cookies out of the oven. Point out that the sentence states that "Sylvia rushed into the kitchen." Students cannot conclude that Sylvia was baking the cookies, although they could infer this, because the sentence gives no evidence to support that conclusion. Perhaps another family member or friend was baking the cookies. Remind students that the conclusion they draw must be supported by the information in the selection in order to be a correct or logical conclusion.

How the Lessons Are Organized

Each lesson contains three or four short reading selections for which students are asked to choose a conclusion that can logically be drawn from the information presented. Lessons 7 through 12 are more difficult because students are asked to identify a conclusion that cannot be drawn from the information presented.

Practice Activity

Read this story to your students.

In 1958 there was an earthquake in Springhill, Canada. There were 69 men trapped in the mine near town. The rescue workers dug fast and hard. But by the sixth day, few family members came to the mine. The sad rescue workers shook their heads but kept on digging. Then a voice was heard through an air pipe. "There are 12 of us in here. Please rescue us."

From the story you can tell that
  A. Springhill was a big city
  B. the people thought the men were dead
  C. it was snowing during the earthquake
  D. no one cared about the miners

Remind students to read all the clues in the story. They should find a conclusion that fits all the clues. To make sure that they find the correct conclusion, they should ask, "How do I know this?" They should know because of the clues in the story.

OVERVIEW: INFERENCE

Introducing the Skill

Have students imagine that they are at a friend's house. Tell them there is a cake with candles on one table and many presents on another. Balloons and crepe-paper streamers hang from the ceiling. There are many people there. Ask students to make an inference about why this is a special day for their friend. Discuss what facts and personal knowledge or experiences lead them to infer that their friend is having a birthday party. Remind students that they can make inferences by thinking about what they already know and including it with the facts given in the reading selection. Point out that facts can be found in the selection but that the inference cannot.

How the Lessons Are Organized

A lesson consists of three or four short reading selections. Lessons 1 through 6 ask students to choose one logical inference that can be made from the information presented in each selection. Lessons 7 through 12 practice the skill at a more difficult level. Factual and inferential statements follow each reading selection. Students must differentiate the facts in the selection from the inferences that can logically be made.

Practice Activity

Read these stories to your students.

> Will was a baby and only knew a few words. One day he pointed to a dog and said, "Dog!" His mother praised him for learning a new word. The next day Will pointed to a cat and said, "Dog!" Later a squirrel ran by. Will pointed and shouted, "Dog!"

Which of these sentences is probably true?
A. Will wanted his bottle.
B. Will was afraid of dogs.
C. Will thought that all small animals were dogs.
D. Will liked cats better than squirrels.

> Pigs are smart. They can learn many tricks. They can fetch sticks, dance, and tumble. It takes a pig less time than a dog to learn tricks. Pigs like people and are very curious. Pigs can even learn to open gates and locks.

Choose whether each statement is an inference or a fact.

Fact	Inference	
O	O	A. Pigs can learn to open locks. (F)
O	O	B. Pigs can learn many tricks. (F)
O	O	C. Pigs are smarter than dogs. (I)
O	O	D. Pigs are curious. (F)

Remind students to keep in mind the difference between facts and inferences. They should think about the facts in the story and what they already know. Encourage them to make an inference by putting together what they know and what they read.

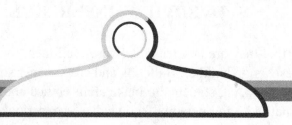

Dear Parent:

During this school year, our class will be working on a variety of reading skills. We will be completing activity sheets that provide practice in the comprehension skills that can help your child become a better reader. The skills we will be focusing on are: finding the facts, detecting a sequence, learning new vocabulary through context, identifying the main idea, drawing conclusions, and making inferences.

From time to time, I may send home activity sheets. To best help your child, please consider the following suggestions:

- Provide a quiet place to work.
- Go over the directions together.
- Encourage your child to do his or her best.
- Check the lesson when it is complete.
- Go over your child's work and note improvements as well as problems.

Help your child maintain a positive attitude about reading. Provide as many opportunities for reading with your child as possible. Read books from the library, comics in the newspaper, and even cereal boxes. Let your child know that these activities provide an opportunity to have fun and to learn. Above all, enjoy this time you spend with your child. He or she will feel your support, and skills will improve with each activity completed.

Thank you for your help!

Cordially,

Name _____   Date _____

Secret Sharks

Read the story. Choose the answer that best completes each sentence.

Most people think of sharks as the ones they see in the movies. These "movie stars" are usually the great white sharks. However, the great whites are just one of 350 kinds of sharks. There are some sharks that have never been seen alive. They live deep in the ocean. They are like the sharks that lived three hundred million years ago.

One example is the goblin shark. It lives hundreds of feet under the sea. Scientists do not believe that it could live if it came to the ocean surface. People in Japan have built a small submarine to learn more about goblin sharks.

Another unusual shark is the megamouth. *Mega* means large and strong. One megamouth that scientists have seen was fifteen feet long. Its mouth was four feet long.

_____

_____ 1. The sharks usually seen in movies are
   A. gray sharks   C. megamouth sharks
   B. goblin sharks   D. great white sharks

_____ 2. How many kinds of sharks are there?
   A. 300   C. 4,500
   B. 15   D. 350

_____ 3. The goblin shark will be studied using a
   A. submarine   C. library
   B. telescope   D. museum

_____ 4. *Mega* means large and
   A. mean   C. strong
   B. rare   D. hungry

_____ 5. The mouth of one megamouth was about
   A. three feet long   C. fifteen feet long
   B. four feet long   D. sixty feet long

Go on to the next page.

Name_____   Date _____

Scientists are trying to learn more about other unusual sharks. One is the frilled shark. This creature has a body like an eel. It has frills on its neck. Scientists want to know what the frilled shark eats. They think it may eat squid.

There are many amazing kinds of small sharks, too. The cookie-cutter shark is only sixteen inches long, but it has very large teeth. This shark also has strong lips. It holds a larger fish with its lips while it scoops out big bites.

Many small sharks hunt together. This way they can kill fish much larger than themselves. One kind of shark that does this is the cigar shark. You can probably guess how this shark got its name. It is the size and shape of a cigar. It is even small enough for you to hold in your hand!

_____

_____ **6.** Scientists are studying
     A. large sharks   **C.** unusual sharks
     B. unkind sharks   **D.** common sharks

_____ **7.** The shark that looks like an eel is the
     A. cigar shark   **C.** eel shark
     B. goblin shark   **D.** frilled shark

_____ **8.** The cookie-cutter shark is
     A. little   **C.** tasty
     B. huge   **D.** fishy

_____ **9.** The cookie-cutter shark has strong
     A. cookies   **C.** eyes
     B. fins   **D.** lips

_____ **10.** One shark that hunts in groups is the
     A. goblin shark   **C.** frilled shark
     B. cigar shark   **D.** ghost shark

Name_____   Date _____

Beard Beginnings

Read the story. Choose the answer that best completes each sentence.

There's nothing really new about beards. Men have been growing beards for thousands of years. If a man does not shave his chin and the sides of his face, a beard will grow. Long ago all men had beards.

The first men to shave off their beards were the early Egyptians. But not all Egyptian men shaved. Some spent hours caring for their beards. They dyed them, braided them, and even wove gold threads into them. The kings and queens of Egypt sometimes wore false beards called postiches. A postiche was a sign of royalty. It was made of metal and attached to the chin with straps of gold.

Some men in ancient Greece wore beards. They thought a beard was a sign of wisdom. Socrates was a famous Greek who wore a beard. He was also thought to be a wise man.

_____ **1.** If a man doesn't shave, he will grow a
   A. nose   C. braid
   B. beard   D. chin

_____ **2.** Long ago all men had
   A. postiches   C. gold
   B. beards   D. wisdom

_____ **3.** The kings of Egypt sometimes wore
   A. false beards   C. diamond beards
   B. wise beards   D. cloth beards

_____ **4.** A postiche was a sign of
   A. weakness   C. royalty
   B. loyalty   D. marriage

_____ **5.** A famous Greek who wore a beard was
   A. Postiche   C. Egyptian
   B. Burnside   D. Socrates

Go on to the next page.

Name_____   Date _____

For hundreds of years, beards were not popular. They became fashionable again in the 1500s. One style of beard was called the goatee. This small, pointed beard hangs from the lower lip and chin. It looks like the beard of a goat. In the 1600s another style of beard became popular. It was called the Vandyke. This beard was named after a famous painter of the time, Anthony Vandyke.

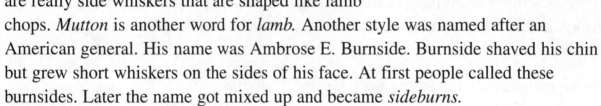

Men wore their whiskers in still other ways in the 1800s. Some men wore muttonchops. These are really side whiskers that are shaped like lamb chops. *Mutton* is another word for *lamb*. Another style was named after an American general. His name was Ambrose E. Burnside. Burnside shaved his chin but grew short whiskers on the sides of his face. At first people called these burnsides. Later the name got mixed up and became *sideburns*.

_____ **6.** The goatee became the fashion in the
  A. 1400s   **C.** 1700s
  B. 1500s   **D.** 1800s

_____ **7.** The Vandyke beard was named after a
  A. general   **C.** painter
  B. king   **D.** lamb

_____ **8.** Muttonchops are really
  A. postiches   **C.** chin whiskers
  B. lambs   **D.** side whiskers

_____ **9.** Sideburns were named for an American
  A. officer   **C.** lamb chop
  B. artist   **D.** mutton

_____ **10.** Sideburns were popular in the
  A. 1500s   **C.** 1700s
  B. 1600s   **D.** 1800s

Name_____   Date _____

Pretty Pearls

Read the story. Choose the answer that best completes each sentence.

Down, down go the divers. At the bottom of the sea, they pick up oysters that grow there. The divers bring the oysters up to the surface of the water. Other workers then put the oysters into wire baskets. These baskets hang from floating rafts. The oysters float safely in the baskets in the sea.

When the oysters are three years old, they are removed from the sea. Experts put tiny round beads inside the oysters. Then the oysters are returned in their baskets to the sea. From time to time, workers pull the baskets out of the sea. They clean off moss and seaweed from the oyster shells.

Why do the oysters receive such good care? In a few years, the oyster will cover the bead with a shiny coating. It will then become a pearl.

_____ 1. An oyster grows at the bottom of the
    A. sea   C. pearl
    B. raft   D. basket

_____ 2. Oysters are put into wire baskets that
    A. hang   C. sink
    B. swim   D. dive

_____ 3. A bead is put inside the oyster when it is
    A. found   C. three years old
    B. cleaned   D. two years old

_____ 4. From time to time, workers
    A. sell oysters   C. taste oysters
    B. open oysters   D. clean oysters

_____ 5. The bead inside an oyster becomes a
    A. plant   C. ruby
    B. moss   D. pearl

Go on to the next page.

Name_____   Date _____

The story of pearls goes back to 2206 B.C. That is more than four thousand years ago. At that time people in China gave pearls as gifts or rewards. In Persia pearls were used to decorate clay pots. In many countries people thought of pearls as jewels of love. Husbands gave them to their wives. Kings and queens gave them to one another.

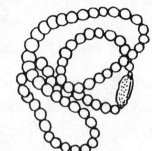

Over the years people have used pearls in many ways. They have decorated crowns and swords with them. They have sewn pearls into fine clothing. Most often people have used pearls in pins, necklaces, rings, and bracelets.

The pearl is the birthstone for people who are born in June. The pearl is said to stand for health, wealth, and a long life. Perhaps that is why many people say that pearls become more beautiful with age.

_____ **6.** Early Chinese people gave pearls as
      A. presents   **C.** kings
      B. baskets   **D.** birthstones

_____ **7.** Long ago in Persia, pearls were used on
      A. walls   **C.** oysters
      B. gifts   **D.** pottery

_____ **8.** People often use pearls in
      A. pottery   **C.** jewelry
      B. flowers   **D.** baskets

_____ **9.** Pearls are birthstones for the month of
      A. April   **C.** July
      B. June   **D.** December

_____ **10.** As pearls age, many people think they are
      A. more costly   **C.** less valuable
      B. less helpful   **D.** more lovely

Name _____   Date _____

Shivering Is Not Just Quivering

Read the story. Choose the answer that best completes each sentence.

Have you ever shivered on a cold day? You may not have noticed, but as you shivered, your body warmed up. Shivering is one way your body stays warm. It happens when signals are sent from the nervous system to the muscles. This is how it works.

The nervous system has two parts. One part is the nerves. They look like long, thin threads. Their job is to carry messages to all parts of the body. The spinal cord and the brain make up the other part of the nervous system. The spinal cord is a large bundle of nerves inside the backbone. Signals from the brain travel down the spinal cord. They go to the rest of the body through the nerves. Muscles receive these signals.

_____ **1.** Shivering helps your body
   A. keep calm   C. cool down
   B. stay warm   D. stand up straight

_____ **2.** Signals go from the nervous system to
   A. the muscles   C. the legs
   B. a certain cell   D. the nerves

_____ **3.** The nervous system has
   A. one part   C. two parts
   B. three parts   D. many parts

_____ **4.** Nerves look like
   A. muscles   C. blood cells
   B. threads   D. small trees

_____ **5.** The spinal cord is a large bundle of
   A. muscles   C. nerves
   B. brain cells   D. signals

Go on to the next page.

Name _____   Date _____

Imagine waiting for a bus on a street corner. It's a cold day, the bus is late, and you feel chilled. Here's what happens.

A control center in your brain senses that you're cold. It sends a message down the spinal cord to all the nerves. The message races through nerves that connect to other nerves. Then it goes from the nerves to the muscles. The message says, "Warning! Prepare for action!"

When a muscle moves, it makes heat. That is why you get warm when you run or play soccer. When your muscles get the signal that you are cold, they get busy. First they become tight, then they loosen. They tighten then loosen over and over again. This makes you shiver. You also get warmer.

_____ **6.** Your brain's signal travels first to the
     A. bus   **C.** heart
     B. spinal cord   **D.** muscles

_____ **7.** Nerves tell the muscles to
     A. stop   **C.** get ready
     B. relax   **D.** cool down

_____ **8.** When a muscle moves, it becomes
     A. warm   **C.** stiff
     B. cool   **D.** heavy

_____ **9.** When you become cold, your muscles
     A. relax   **C.** stop moving
     B. stretch   **D.** tighten and loosen

_____ **10.** When you shiver, you get
     A. weaker   **C.** stronger
     B. colder   **D.** warmer

Go on to the next page.

Name _____   Date _____

Bring More Water, Molly Pitcher

Read the story. Choose the answer that best completes each sentence.

Molly Ludwig was a young girl when she met John Hays. She married him before she turned 15. They lived a quiet life in Pennsylvania. John worked as a barber, and Molly took care of their son.

Then their peaceful life changed. Many people felt that it was time for America to win its freedom from British rule. Along with his friends and neighbors, John joined the army.

Molly followed John into war. Like many young wives of the day, she washed and cooked for him while he fought in the war. She and John put up with the hardships of army life for three years.

_____ **1.** Molly married John before she was
      A. 19   **C.** 15
      B. 14   **D.** 20

_____ **2.** John worked as a
      A. lawyer   **C.** saddle maker
      B. doctor   **D.** barber

_____ **3.** Many people felt America should
      A. make laws   **C.** win its freedom
      B. make money   **D.** collect taxes

_____ **4.** John joined the
      A. British   **C.** local club
      B. army   **D.** barber school

_____ **5.** While John fought the war, Molly
      A. rode horses   **C.** laughed and played
      B. visited friends   **D.** washed and cooked

Go on to the next page.

Name _____   Date _____

Molly was given a nickname by George Washington's troops. She hauled water to the men as they fought in battles. She carried the water in pitchers. One hot day as the men drank the cool water, they gave Molly her new name. They called her Molly Pitcher.

As she worked, Molly watched John fight. He was forcing cannonballs into a cannon with a long pole. All at once she saw him fall to the ground. She could tell he was hurt as he was moved off the field. Molly rushed to take his place at the cannon. She grabbed the pole and started to work. The battle went on as Molly fought in John's place. After the battle Molly joined the army. She served as a soldier for almost eight years.

_____ **6.** Molly earned her nickname by hauling

    A. water   **C.** cannons

    B. logs   **D.** meat

_____ **7.** Molly helped the soldiers during

    A. meals   **C.** illness

    B. marches   **D.** battles

_____ **8.** John put cannonballs in the cannon with

    A. a door   **C.** a pitcher

    B. water   **D.** a long pole

_____ **9.** When John fell, Molly took his

    A. pitcher   **C.** place

    B. horse   **D.** hat

_____ **10.** After the battle Molly became a

    A. teacher   **C.** nurse

    B. soldier   **D.** pilot

Go on to the next page.

Name_____   Date _____

Made for the Job

Read the story. Choose the answer that best completes each sentence.

If you looked at a bald eagle, it would stare back at you. But the eagle would see you more clearly than you see it. Birds can see better than other animals. And eagles can see better than other birds. An eagle can see three to eight times better than a human can. This helps it with its main job, hunting. While an eagle glides high in the air, it can spot a fish in a stream far below.

An eagle must fly great distances in search of food. Its wings also help it hunt. When an eagle's wings are spread out, they stretch out six or seven feet. These large wings can carry an eagle over a hundred miles in a day.

_____ **1.** If you looked at a bald eagle, it would
  A. squawk   C. fly away
  B. blink   D. stare back

_____ **2.** An eagle's sharp eyes help it
  A. sleep   C. find a mate
  B. hunt   D. fly

_____ **3.** While it is flying, an eagle looks for
  A. food   C. feathers
  B. humans   D. other eagles

_____ **4.** An eagle's wings can measure
  A. three feet   C. fifteen feet
  B. five feet   D. seven feet

_____ **5.** In a day an eagle can fly more than
  A. 600 miles   C. 100 miles
  B. 700 miles   D. 1,000 miles

Go on to the next page.

Name_____   Date _____

When a hungry eagle sees a fish, it swoops down at top speed toward the stream. Then it snatches the fish with its sharp claws. These claws are called talons. The talons are at least one inch long. They grasp the fish tightly as the eagle soars upward. The toes and the bottoms of the eagle's feet are covered with hundreds of tiny bumps. These bumps help it hold the slippery fish.

The eagle might carry the fish to shore. There the eagle's pointed beak helps it eat the fish. An eagle uses its beak to catch prey and to tear meat.

_____ **6.** When a hungry eagle sees a fish, it
A. calls out   C. flies higher
B. dives   D. flies away

_____ **7.** An eagle picks up its food with its
A. feet   C. eyes
B. wings   D. feathers

_____ **8.** An eagle's talons
A. help it see   C. help it fly
B. are not sharp   D. catch its food

_____ **9.** The tiny bumps on an eagle's feet help it
A. fly   C. hold its food
B. see   D. soar upward

_____ **10.** An eagle's pointed beak helps it to
A. fly   C. crack seeds
B. eat   D. grab branches

Go on to the next page.

Name_____   Date _____

Louis Braille

Read the story. Choose the answer that best completes each sentence.

Louis Braille was born in a small French town. When he was three, he lost his sight. At ten he went to a school for children who were blind. The books at his school were written with raised letters. He moved his fingers over the letters to read the books. But letters like *A* and *H* felt the same. He had a hard time understanding what he read.

Then Louis learned of a different way to read. It was used by soldiers who had to read messages in the dark. To write the messages, people punched dots in paper. Since the dots were raised, people could feel them.

Braille Alphabet

a	b	c	d	e	f	g	h	i	j
1	2	3	4	5	6	7	8	9	0

k	l	m	n	o	p	q	r	s	t

u	v	w	x	y	z	Capital Sign	Numeral Sign

_____   **1.** Louis Braille was born in

     A. Spain   **C.** England

     B. France   **D.** the United States

_____   **2.** Louis lost his sight when he was

     A. two   **C.** ten

     B. three   **D.** fifteen

_____   **3.** To read books Louis used

     A. his fingers   **C.** a machine

     B. his eyes   **D.** his mother's help

_____   **4.** Louis had a hard time understanding

     A. his friends   **C.** what he heard

     B. his teachers   **D.** what he read

_____   **5.** The system with raised dots was used by

     A. miners   **C.** doctors

     B. soldiers   **D.** forest rangers

Go on to the next page.

Name_____ Date _____

Louis liked the idea of reading with raised dots. But he thought it could be made simpler. So when Louis was fifteen, he made up a new way of writing. He used raised dots, but he made up his own alphabet.

All of Louis's friends at school liked his idea. But many teachers did not want to use it. They thought the old way worked just fine. Then in 1844 this new way of reading and writing was shown to the public. When more people saw how it worked, they liked it. Today people all over the world read books written in Braille.

_____ **6.** Louis decided to use the idea of reading

    A. old books   **C.** raised dots

    B. aloud   **D.** picture books

_____ **7.** Louis's new system used

    A. small letters   **C.** no raised dots

    B. a machine   **D.** a new alphabet

_____ **8.** Louis's friends thought his system

    A. was strange   **C.** worked well

    B. was too hard   **D.** did not work

_____ **9.** At first the new system was not used by

    A. parents   **C.** the government

    B. students   **D.** people who taught school

_____ **10.** Today Braille's system

    A. is not used   **C.** does not work

    B. is well liked   **D.** is used only in France

Name _____   Date _____

Abe's "Tall" Tale

Abe Lincoln was the sixteenth president of the United States.
He was a very tall man. He had black hair that would not stay
down when he combed it. His thin arms were long and strong.
Lincoln was a serious man, but he also had a funny side. He
was famous for his jokes and funny stories.

When Abe began to grow tall as a boy, his stepmother teased him about his height.
She would tell him to keep the top of his head clean. That way he wouldn't get her
ceiling dirty. She told him that it was easy enough to wash the floor when it got dirty,
but the ceiling was another matter.

Abe took this teasing in good spirits. He didn't mind being tall. Besides, there wasn't
much he could do about it.

Then one day Abe got an idea. He was watching some little boys playing in the
mud. He noticed how dirty their feet were. Abe looked around. His stepmother
wasn't home. So he went outside toward the boys in the mud puddle. He picked up
one boy and carried him into the house. Then he went back and picked up another
boy.

One by one, Abe turned the boys upside down. Then he walked their dirty feet
across the clean, white ceiling. They made a trail of muddy footprints from one
room to the other. The boys thought this was great fun, and so did Abe.

Then Abe waited for his stepmother to return. When she did, she saw the
footprints right away. "Abe Lincoln, you've played a good joke on me!" she
laughed. "I guess I deserve it."

When the laughter was over, Abe got the paintbrush out. He put a fresh coat of
paint on the ceiling that made it cleaner and brighter than ever before.

Go on to the next page.

Name _____   Date _____

Choose the phrase that best answers each question.

1. Put these events in the order that they happened. What happened first? Write the number **1** on the line by that sentence. Then write the number **2** by the sentence that tells what happened next. Write the number **3** by the sentence that tells what happened last.

_____ Abe's stepmother teased him.

_____ Abe brought the boys into the house.

_____ Abe saw some little boys playing in the mud.

_____ 2. When did Abe carry the boys into the house?

    A. when he saw them playing outside in the mud

    B. after he walked their feet across the ceiling

    C. before he looked to see if his stepmother was around

_____ 3. When Abe's stepmother returned, what did she do?

    A. She saw the footprints.

    B. She painted the ceiling.

    C. She left.

_____ 4. When did Abe get the paintbrush out?

    A. after he became president

    B. before he saw the boys in the mud

    C. after he played the joke on his stepmother

_____ 5. When did this story take place?

    A. while Abe was president

    B. before Abe was president

    C. after Abe was president

Name _____   **Date** _____

Making Chocolate Candy

A chocolate candy bar is easy to eat, but it is hard to make. Chocolate fruits grow on trees in countries where the climate is hot. The fruits grow on the trunks of the trees. When these fruits are as big as bowling balls, workers cut them down. Workers split the shells and remove the chocolate beans. They lay the beans outside in the sun and cover them with banana leaves. Later, workers uncover the beans to dry them. When the beans are very dry, workers put them in bags. These bags of beans are sent to other countries to be made into candy.

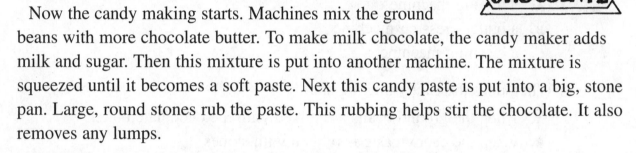

First the candy maker uses machines to clean the dry beans. Next the beans are heated and ground. Huge machines press a chocolate butter from these ground beans.

Now the candy making starts. Machines mix the ground beans with more chocolate butter. To make milk chocolate, the candy maker adds milk and sugar. Then this mixture is put into another machine. The mixture is squeezed until it becomes a soft paste. Next this candy paste is put into a big, stone pan. Large, round stones rub the paste. This rubbing helps stir the chocolate. It also removes any lumps.

After hours of rubbing, the candy is almost ready. Fruits or nuts may be added now. The candy is made into bars. When the bars have cooled, they are wrapped. They are then packed and sent to the stores.

Go on to the next page.

Name _____   Date _____

Choose the phrase that best answers each question.

1. Put these events in the order that they happened. What happened first? Write the number **1** on the line by that sentence. Then write the number **2** by the sentence that tells what happened next. Write the number **3** by the sentence that tells what happened last.

   _____ Workers dry the beans.

   _____ Workers take the beans out of their shells.

   _____ Workers put the beans in bags.

_____ 2. Which machine are the chocolate beans put into first?
   A. a mixing machine
   B. a butter-pressing machine
   C. a cleaning machine

_____ 3. When does the candy making start?
   A. when the ground beans are mixed with the chocolate butter
   B. when the candy paste is rubbed with stones
   C. when the candy is shaped into bars

_____ 4. When are fruits or nuts added to the chocolate bars?
   A. when the bars are wrapped for shipping
   B. before the candy is shaped into bars
   C. while the candy is being cleaned

_____ 5. When is the candy sent to the stores?
   A. while the candy is cooling
   B. before the candy has been wrapped
   C. after the candy has been packed

Name_____   Date _____

Trapped!

It was December 1984. A large herd of hungry white whales was chasing codfish. The whales chased the codfish from the sea into the Senyavin Strait. This narrow body of water separates an island from the coast of Russia.

An angry east wind blew. The water began to freeze. Soon the strait was jammed with ice that was up to twelve feet thick. Only small pools of open water remained. The whales were trapped in the strait!

A hunter spotted the whales and saw that they were in trouble. White whales can break through thin ice, but this ice was too thick. The hunter knew that whales must rise to the water's surface in order to breathe. There just wasn't enough room for thousands of these ten-foot whales to breathe. Soon there were helicopters on the scene. They dropped frozen fish to feed the whales. But the whales still could not breathe. They were beginning to die. The helpers sent for a special ship. Spotter planes helped the ship find the right place in which to ram through the ice. At first the whales just rested in the big pools that the ship made. Then as the whales became stronger, they began to play.

This was not what the captain of the ship wanted. He knew that the water would freeze again. Somehow he had to get the whales to follow the ship out to sea. Finally someone remembered that porpoises like music. Whales are related to porpoises. Maybe they would like music, too. So the crew of the ship played all kinds of music on deck. The whales liked classical music best.

Slowly they began to follow the ship. It took a long time to get the whales out of the strait. The ship would break the ice and then wait for the whales. After a while the whales got used to the ship. They swam around the ship on all sides. By February the white whales were safely in the sea again.

Go on to the next page.

Name _____   Date _____

Choose the phrase that best answers each question.

1. Put these events in the order that they happened. What happened first? Write the number **1** on the line by that sentence. Then write the number **2** by the sentence that tells what happened next. Write the number **3** by the sentence that tells what happened last.

   _____ The whales were trapped.

   _____ The east wind blew.

   _____ The whales entered the strait.

_____ 2. When were the whales trapped?
   A. after they followed the codfish
   B. before December
   C. after the icebreaker arrived

_____ 3. When did the ship arrive?
   A. after helicopters flew over
   B. while the whales played
   C. after the thick ice had melted

_____ 4. What did the special ship do first?
   A. It led the whales to safety.
   B. It played classical music.
   C. It rammed the ice.

_____ 5. When were the whales in the strait?
   A. from December to February
   B. from Saturday through Friday
   C. from February to December

Name _____   Date _____

Sequoyah

Sequoyah's people, the Cherokees, did not know how to write. They did not have an alphabet. They could not read books. Sequoyah wanted to draw some letters for the Cherokees.

First he drew pictures on tree bark. He needed a new picture for each word. He was so busy that he had no time to hunt. His garden of corn and beans died. One day Sequoyah's wife burned all his bark pictures. Sequoyah became very angry. He took his daughter, Ah-Yoka, and went away.

Later the two found a book written in English. Sequoyah saw that there were only 26 different marks. He realized that he didn't need a picture for each word. He just needed a mark for each sound. So he started all over again.

Finally the work was done. He taught the letters to Ah-Yoka. Then he talked to the Cherokee leaders about his work. They did not believe him. They wanted to test the letters.

The leaders told Sequoyah, "You go away for a little while. We will talk with your daughter. Then she will write a letter to you. When you return, you must read the letter to us. The words must be the words we told your daughter." Sequoyah was worried. Ah-Yoka was only ten years old. He went away and waited.

Later the leaders called him back. He picked up the letter and read the words out loud. The words were the same words that the leaders had used. Sequoyah's idea had worked!

Go on to the next page.

Name _____   Date _____

Choose the phrase that best answers each question.

1. Put these events in the order that they happened. What happened first? Write the number **1** on the line by that sentence. Then write the number **2** by the sentence that tells what happened next. Write the number **3** by the sentence that tells what happened last.

   _____ Ah-Yoka wrote down the words of the leaders.

   _____ Sequoyah read Ah-Yoka's letter.

   _____ The leaders talked with Ah-Yoka.

_____ 2. When did Ah-Yoka and Sequoyah find a book written in English?

   A. after Sequoyah moved away from his wife
   B. before he started drawing pictures for words
   C. after the Cherokee leaders sent him away

_____ 3. When did Ah-Yoka write a letter to Sequoyah?

   A. before he saw the marks in English
   B. before his wife got angry at him
   C. after he talked with the Cherokee leaders

_____ 4. When did the leaders think that Sequoyah's idea could work?

   A. before his wife burned the bark pictures
   B. after he read Ah-Yoka's letter
   C. before the leaders talked with Ah-Yoka

_____ 5. When did Sequoyah realize that he needed only a mark for each sound?

   A. before he drew pictures on tree bark
   B. after he taught the letters to Ah-Yoka
   C. after he saw 26 marks in English

Name_____   Date _____

The Space Shuttle

To shuttle means to go back and forth. The space shuttle was designed to go back and forth between Earth and space. The first shuttle flight was on April 12, 1981.

The space shuttle has four main parts. It has an orbiter, a fuel tank, and two rocket boosters. The orbiter is like an airplane. It carries the crew. It has its own engines. The orbiter is the part of the shuttle that goes all the way around Earth.

The orbiter is attached to a huge tank. This tank holds fuel for its engines. On each side of the tank is a rocket booster. These rockets fire up on liftoff. In two minutes they run out of fuel. They fall from the orbiter. Parachutes slow their fall to the sea. Then boats tow the rockets to shore. The rockets can be used again as many as twenty times.

After eight minutes the big tank runs out of fuel. It falls and breaks into pieces over the sea. Now only the orbiter is left. It enters its orbit in space. It may have as many as seven crew members on board. Often the crew members launch satellites. Sometimes they work on experiments.

When it is time to come back to Earth, the orbiter's engines are fired. This slows the spacecraft down. It drops from orbit. Tiles protect the shuttle from the heat caused by entering Earth's atmosphere. The spacecraft now acts like a plane. The shuttle glides to a landing on a runway.

Go on to the next page.

Comprehension 4, SV 6186-9

Name _____   Date _____

Choose the phrase that best answers each question.

1. Put these events in the order that they happened. What happened first? Write the number **1** on the line by that sentence. Then write the number **2** by the sentence that tells what happened next. Write the number **3** by the sentence that tells what happened last.

   _____ The shuttle drops from orbit.

   _____ The orbiter's engines are fired.

   _____ The shuttle glides to a landing.

_____ 2. When do the rockets fire up?
   A. while the orbiter is circling Earth
   B. right before landing
   C. at liftoff

_____ 3. When do the rockets run out of fuel?
   A. after two minutes
   B. after they fall from the orbiter
   C. on the runway

_____ 4. When does the orbiter enter its orbit?
   A. before dawn
   B. after the big fuel tank falls to the sea
   C. after 14 hours

_____ 5. When do the orbiter's engines slow it down?
   A. when the shuttle is ready to return to Earth
   B. before it reaches orbit
   C. at liftoff

Name_____   Date _____

Black Widow Spiders

Did you know that the black widow spider is one of the most poisonous spiders in the world? But only the females can hurt you. The males are harmless. The female's poison is much stronger than that of a rattlesnake. A person who has been bitten can die if he or she does not get treatment.

The female black widow is about half an inch long. She is black and has red marks on her belly. The black widow gets her name from the fact that she sometimes eats her mate. The male is one-third of the female's size. He doesn't have any red marks.

Let's observe one black widow female. When we first see her, she is hanging upside down in her web. She stays there for three days without moving. Her skin becomes too small, so she sheds it. She grows a new, larger skin. This is called molting, and it happens about eight times during her life.

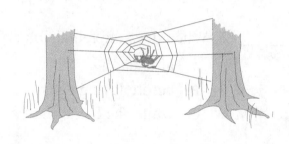

One day a male black widow comes to the edge of the female's web. He strums on the web. If the female is ready to mate, she will strum also. If not, she might chase and eat him. It is dangerous to be a male black widow.

After mating, the female weaves a small, silk sac. This is where she will lay 250 to 750 eggs. Black widows lay their eggs in the spring. The female guards the egg sac for about a month. Then baby spiders, or spiderlings, hatch. The spiderlings are small and helpless when they come out of the egg sac. Many are eaten by birds or insects. Some are even eaten by their mother. Most, however, live and become adults.

Go on to the next page.

Name _____ Date _____

Choose the phrase that best answers each question.

1. Put these events in the order that they happened. What happened first? Write the number **1** on the line by that sentence. Then write the number **2** by the sentence that tells what happened next. Write the number **3** by the sentence that tells what happened last.

    _____ The spiderlings hatch.

    _____ The female makes the egg sac.

    _____ The male black widow strums on the web.

_____ 2. When does the female black widow hang in her web without moving?
    A. after eating
    B. before laying eggs
    C. while she is molting

_____ 3. When does the female black widow strum on her web?
    A. when she is ready to mate
    B. when she is hungry
    C. when she is sleepy

_____ 4. When does the female make an egg sac?
    A. when she is molting
    B. after mating
    C. before biting someone

_____ 5. When do black widows lay their eggs?
    A. in the spring
    B. during summer
    C. before the first snow

Name _____   Date _____

Mary McLeod Bethune

Today almost all children in the United States go to school. But this was not always true. In the 1880s there were few schools for African Americans. This was the case in South Carolina, where Mary McLeod lived.

Mary McLeod was one of 17 children. Her whole family had to work hard to make ends meet. Mary picked cotton in the fields. But she dreamed of learning to read. When she was nine, her dream came true. A church opened a school. Mr. McLeod could spare only one child. He sent Mary. Mary studied hard for the next three years. She loved school.

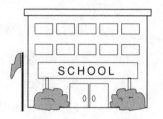

But there was no high school for African Americans in the area where Mary lived. A woman gave Mary money so that she could go away to school. She spent the next seven years in Scotia, a school in North Carolina. She graduated in 1894. Mary spent the rest of her life giving back the gift of education she had received. She taught in small towns for eight years. During this time she met and married Albertus Bethune.

Mary loved teaching. But she dreamed of having her own school. In 1904 she moved to Florida. There she opened a school for girls. In two years she had two hundred and fifty girls and four teachers. It was hard to keep the school open. There were never enough funds.

In 1923 her school joined with a boys' school. Its new name was Bethune-Cookman College. Mary was the president of this school until 1942. She became known as a leader and received many awards. From 1935 to 1944, she served as an advisor to President Roosevelt.

Go on to the next page.

Name_____   Date _____

Choose the phrase that best answers each question.

1. Put these events in the order that they happened. What happened first? Write the number **1** on the line by that sentence. Then write the number **2** by the sentence that tells what happened next. Write the number **3** by the sentence that tells what happened last.

_____ Mary's school joined with a boys' school.

_____ Mary picked cotton in the fields.

_____ Mary married Albertus Bethune.

_____ 2. When did Mary begin going to school?

    A. before she was six

    B. after she was twelve

    C. when she was nine

_____ 3. When did Mary graduate from Scotia?

    A. in 1894

    B. when she was 12

    C. in May 1898

_____ 4. When did Mary open her own school?

    A. before she got married

    B. after she moved to Florida

    C. when she lived in North Carolina

_____ 5. When did Mary serve as an advisor to President Roosevelt?

    A. from 1935 to 1944

    B. when she was 35

    C. when she graduated from Scotia

Name_____   Date _____

Read the stories. Choose the word that best completes each sentence.

People in Russia give eggs as gifts. They do not give just plain white eggs. The eggs are painted with pictures. Many of the pictures have __(1)__ meanings, such as "good luck" and "long life." In Russia __(2)__ eggs become little works of art!

_____ **1. A.** special   **B.** cold   **C.** small   **D.** purple

_____ **2. A.** lizard   **B.** ordinary   **C.** red   **D.** broken

---

A man wondered whether bees know which flowers to go to. So he drew flowers on a large __(3)__ of paper. Half the flowers were blue. The other half were yellow. On each blue flower, he put a big cup of sugar water. But he put a __(4)__ cup on each yellow flower. The bees stopped going to the yellow flowers.

_____ **3. A.** test   **B.** row   **C.** sheet   **D.** pencil

_____ **4. A.** big   **B.** tiny   **C.** glass   **D.** slow

---

Some plants don't have seeds. So how can you grow a seedless grape plant? First cut off a piece of __(5)__ from a grape plant. Put it in water. Soon it begins to grow roots. Plant it in the __(6)__ . It will grow into a new grape plant.

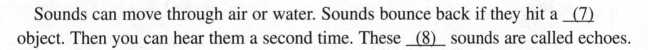

_____ **5. A.** stem   **B.** tree   **C.** spoon   **D.** stone

_____ **6. A.** step   **B.** dirt   **C.** green   **D.** road

---

Sounds can move through air or water. Sounds bounce back if they hit a __(7)__ object. Then you can hear them a second time. These __(8)__ sounds are called echoes.

_____ **7. A.** solid   **B.** mean   **C.** burned   **D.** eager

_____ **8. A.** fair   **B.** forty   **C.** pink   **D.** repeated

Go on to the next page.

Name _____   Date _____

Read the stories. Choose the word that best completes each sentence.

9. Animals have different ways to **escape** from danger. Some run very fast. Others climb trees. But some are safe because they are hard to see. They may be the same color as the ground. Or they may look like plants. They may have stripes or spots that look like the shadows of trees. Instead of running, these animals stand very still.

_____   In this story the word **escape** means
        A. hide   **B.** leave   **C.** chase   **D.** jump

---

10. Every year in Thailand, people have Elephant Day. They bring their elephants to one **location**. Everyone comes to see whose elephant is the best. The elephants run a race. They also carry big logs and stack them in a pile.

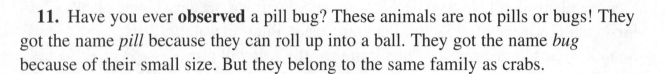

_____   In this story the word **location** means
        A. place   **B.** parade   **C.** street   **D.** country

---

11. Have you ever **observed** a pill bug? These animals are not pills or bugs! They got the name *pill* because they can roll up into a ball. They got the name *bug* because of their small size. But they belong to the same family as crabs.

_____   In this story the word **observed** means
        A. counted   **B.** run   **C.** watched   **D.** cried

---

12. A giant toad finds shelter in a cool, **damp** place. At night the toad comes out. It needs food for its huge appetite. The toad eats as many insects as it can find.

_____   In this story the word **damp** means
        A. dry   **B.** magic   **C.** wet   **D.** shady

Name_____   Date _____

Read the stories. Choose the word that best completes each sentence.

People who like to __(1)__ caves are called spelunkers. To become a spelunker, it is best to begin going with __(2)__ . They take people safely through caves.

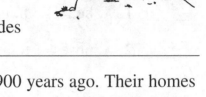

_____ 1. **A.** take   **B.** spin   **C.** explore   **D.** decide

_____ 2. **A.** noises   **B.** surprises   **C.** storms   **D.** guides

_____

The people of South America built beautiful homes 1,900 years ago. Their homes were made of stone. The kitchen was in a __(3)__ building. In the sleeping __(4)__ , the beds were built into a wall.

_____ 3. **A.** mad   **B.** separate   **C.** polite   **D.** fast

_____ 4. **A.** fish   **B.** prairie   **C.** chamber   **D.** farm

_____

Jim Sundberg's bat went whack! The ball flew high above the fielder's glove. It was a home run. Later, people measured the baseball __(5)__ . Someone had drawn the lines wrong. If the lines had been drawn __(6)__ , the hit would have been a foul ball, and the other team may have won.

_____ 5. **A.** cat   **B.** glove   **C.** diamond   **D.** bottom

_____ 6. **A.** alone   **B.** correctly   **C.** wrong   **D.** ugly

_____

Saturn was named for the Roman god of farming. This great __(7)__ is famous for the rings around it. The seven main rings are made up of huge __(8)__ of ice.

_____ 7. **A.** planet   **B.** mud   **C.** club   **D.** pond

_____ 8. **A.** maps   **B.** drinks   **C.** chunks   **D.** tubs

Name _____   Date _____

Read the stories. Choose the word that best completes each sentence.

Totem poles are tall wooden poles with animals painted on them. The animals look __(1)__ . Parts of them look like people. One part of each animal sticks out. Bears have huge claws. Beavers have long front teeth. Crows have long, straight __(2)__ .

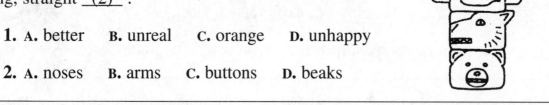

_____ 1. **A.** better   **B.** unreal   **C.** orange   **D.** unhappy

_____ 2. **A.** noses   **B.** arms   **C.** buttons   **D.** beaks

The first Ferris wheel was taller than a twenty-story building. George Ferris made the giant wheel ride for the 1893 World's Fair. It had 36 cars. It held many __(3)__ . At the top of the wheel, everyone could see for __(4)__ .

_____ 3. **A.** passengers   **B.** puppets   **C.** rulers   **D.** balls

_____ 4. **A.** glasses   **B.** animals   **C.** miles   **D.** hours

The numbat has sharp claws on its front feet. The numbat uses these to tear open __(5)__ logs. Then it puts its long, sticky __(6)__ inside to catch termites. A numbat eats only termites.

_____ 5. **A.** yellow   **B.** square   **C.** red   **D.** rotten

_____ 6. **A.** brain   **B.** tongue   **C.** fin   **D.** eye

There is gold in ocean water. The __(7)__ is getting it out. Since the gold there is __(8)__ , taking it out of the ocean costs a lot of money. Maybe one day someone will find an easy way to do it.

_____ 7. **A.** bank   **B.** team   **C.** number   **D.** problem

_____ 8. **A.** scarce   **B.** light   **C.** free   **D.** nickel

Name_____   Date _____

Read the stories. Choose the word that best completes each sentence.

Harriet Tubman was a slave who escaped to __(1)__ in the North. She worried about the slaves still in the South, so she returned many times. Each time, she helped slaves escape. A huge __(2)__ was offered to anyone who caught her. But no one ever did.

_____ **1. A.** nowhere   **B.** rains   **C.** us   **D.** freedom

_____ **2. A.** reward   **B.** trunk   **C.** cave   **D.** seal

---

In the spring some fish leave the __(3)__ where they live. They swim __(4)__ in rivers to ponds where they were born. These fish can find their way even when their eyes are covered. But they get lost if their noses are covered. The fish use their noses to find their way!

_____ **3. A.** ocean   **B.** valley   **C.** basket   **D.** leaf

_____ **4. A.** everywhere   **B.** hardly   **C.** upstream   **D.** here

---

Puffins are birds that live on northern coasts. __(5)__ of puffins stay at sea most of the time. They swim and dive to catch fish. They come on land to nest on high __(6)__ .

_____ **5. A.** Pans   **B.** Friends   **C.** Flocks   **D.** Barns

_____ **6. A.** cliffs   **B.** seas   **C.** nets   **D.** pits

---

Smog is usually a mix of smoke and fog. It can also come from the sun acting on __(7)__ in the air. Smog can __(8)__ a person's health and kill plant life. Smog can be very thick, making it hard to see things.

_____ **7. A.** stars   **B.** fumes   **C.** pals   **D.** pens

_____ **8. A.** fix   **B.** save   **C.** give   **D.** damage

Name _____   Date _____

Read the stories. Choose the word that best completes each sentence.

A magnet can be a piece of stone or metal. Magnets come in a __(1)__ of shapes and sizes. They also come in different __(2)__ , so some are weaker than others.

_____ **1.** A. sack   B. box   C. variety   D. cap

_____ **2.** A. zoos   B. strengths   C. rugs   D. letters

Part of Australia is a huge __(3)__ . People there live hundreds of miles apart. When someone got sick in the past, doctors were too far away to help. Then a group called the Flying Doctors got together. They wanted to __(4)__ sick people. Now doctors use radios for talking to people in need. The doctors use planes to take people to the hospital.

_____ **3.** A. water   B. pan   C. desert   D. street

_____ **4.** A. assist   B. meet   C. forget   D. splash

Many people think we'll live in space one day. Cities will be built inside big glass bubbles. We'll ride in __(5)__ as easily as we now ride in airplanes. Space life sounds very __(6)__ !

_____ **5.** A. horses   B. spaceships   C. land   D. boats

_____ **6.** A. merry   B. quiet   C. exciting   D. poor

A bog starts as a lake, pond, or slow-moving stream. The water gets trapped and can't __(7)__ . This leads to a __(8)__ of moss. Other plants start to die. The mosses and dead plants are a floating mat that becomes a bog.

_____ **7.** A. drain   B. fall   C. care   D. pay

_____ **8.** A. color   B. growth   C. pot   D. fence

Name _____   Date _____

Read the stories. Choose the word that best completes each sentence.

What do you do when you spill salt? Do you throw some over your left side? Once people believed that a bad __(1)__ always stared over their left side. People were afraid that spilling salt would bring bad luck. So they threw the salt over their left side. And that is how this __(2)__ began.

_____ **1.** A. ten   B. card   C. spirit   D. soap

_____ **2.** A. fence   B. custom   C. drink   D. sand

In the 1920s cars were used more and more. They were also starting to go fast. And that meant __(3)__ ! Garrett Morgan made a machine that told drivers when to stop and go. It had __(4)__ red, green, and yellow lights.

_____ **3.** A. accidents   B. nests   C. sets   D. pins

_____ **4.** A. popping   B. flashing   C. eating   D. singing

A fawn lies hidden on the ground in the forest. Its spotted coat helps it stay hidden in the __(5)__ leaves. The fawn will stay very __(6)__ and quiet so it can't be heard by other animals.

_____ **5.** A. fallen   B. burning   C. last   D. thin

_____ **6.** A. lean   B. calm   C. sick   D. loud

Moths are insects with wings. There are many kinds of moths. They live just about everywhere. Moths are a lot like butterflies. It is often __(7)__ to tell them apart. Like butterflies, moths were once __(8)__ .

_____ **7.** A. usual   B. picky   C. difficult   D. tired

_____ **8.** A. rats   B. hens   C. pets   D. caterpillars

Name _____   Date _____

Read the stories. Choose the word that best completes each sentence.

You might think of beavers as the __(1)__ of the animal world. Beavers have strong front teeth. They cut down many trees. Beavers use the branches to build __(2)__ for homes in the water. They use the bark for food.

_____ **1.** **A.** keepers   **B.** lumberjacks
            C. pilots   **D.** knights

_____ **2.** **A.** lodges   **B.** pillows   **C.** motors   **D.** porches

___

The elf owl is most often found in dry areas of the country. It sits still in its nest during the day. Then the owl flies out to feed at __(3)__ . It uses its __(4)__ senses to find food.

_____ **3.** **A.** market   **B.** sundown   **C.** breakfast   **D.** feather

_____ **4.** **A.** flat   **B.** outside   **C.** fat   **D.** keen

___

BOLD is a group that helps blind people learn to ski. The helpers tell how the ski trail looks. They follow the skiers. They say when to turn. They teach other skiing __(5)__ . The blind people ski on the same trails as __(6)__ else.

_____ **5.** **A.** skills   **B.** fiddles   **C.** hairs   **D.** stairs

_____ **6.** **A.** all   **B.** somebody   **C.** everyone   **D.** someone

___

The king or queen of England owns the crown jewels. These __(7)__ include crowns, rings, bracelets, __(8)__ , and swords. They are kept safe in the Tower of London.

_____ **7.** **A.** treasures   **B.** monkeys   **C.** carts   **D.** trails

_____ **8.** **A.** tribes   **B.** doors   **C.** thoughts   **D.** necklaces

Name_____   Date _____

Read the stories. Choose the word or phrase that best completes the sentence.

The ends of our fingers are covered with special lines. The lines are fingerprints. Fingerprints are like rubber **soles** on shoes. The rubber bumps on shoes keep us from falling down. The lines on our fingers help us hold things.

_____ **1.** In this paragraph, the word **soles** means

    A. checks   **C.** bottoms

    B. repairs   **D.** pockets

At first only men could dance on stage. One night a man could not dance. Marie Camargo got on stage and did the man's dance. The people who were watching were **thrilled**. When Camargo finished, they clapped and threw flowers on the stage. Now many stage dancers are women.

_____ **2.** In this paragraph, the word **thrilled** means

    A. delighted   **C.** awakened

    B. upset   **D.** broken

Lodestone is a natural magnet. Long ago, sailors used a piece of lodestone to tell which direction they were going. They tied the stone to a string. They **suspended** the stone in the air. It always pointed to the north.

_____ **3.** In this paragraph, the word **suspended** means

    A. crept   **C.** judged

    B. hung   **D.** grew

The toucan is a brightly colored bird. It makes its home in the Amazon forests. During the day it flies around looking for food. At night it **roosts** in a tree.

_____ **4.** In this paragraph, the word **roosts** means

    A. attacks   **C.** trusts

    B. wastes   **D.** rests

Name_____ Date _____

Read the stories. Choose the word or phrase that best completes the sentence.

Look at the back of a dollar bill. You will find the words *In God We Trust*. This **motto** was first used on a coin. But it wasn't printed on paper money until 1957. Now it is printed on all United States paper money.

_____ **1.** In this paragraph, the word **motto** means

    A. puzzle   C. saying

    B. song   D. money

Fireflies aren't flies at all. They are beetles. These bugs can light up their bodies. The light **flickers** off and on. The flashing light signals other fireflies.

_____ **2.** In this paragraph, the word **flickers** means

    A. swims   C. shadows

    B. laughs   D. shines

The Ringling brothers started a very small circus. At first they did everything themselves. They made tents. They set up the circus acts. This **tough** life helped them become very famous. Now their "Greatest Show on Earth" goes all over the country.

_____ **3.** In this paragraph, the word **tough** means

    A. slow   C. old

    B. hard   D. hungry

The stingray uses its long tail to protect itself. On its tail is a sharp, poison hook. The hook can **pierce** an attacker's skin.

_____ **4.** In this paragraph, the word **pierce** means

    A. change into   C. go through

    B. look around   D. stay beside

Name_____   Date _____

Read the stories. Choose the word or phrase that best completes the sentence.

The roadrunner is a bird. It is one of the fastest hunters in the desert. It can run up to twenty miles an hour. It moves so fast that it can kill a snake. The roadrunner's long legs also help it **flee** from its enemies.

_____ **1.** In this paragraph, the word **flee** means

     A. want   **C.** run

     B. know   **D.** set

A man had been in jail for most of his life. He decided to make a garden. He planted seeds and watered them. As the plants grew, he began to change. He changed from a **bitter** man to a very peaceful man. He said that working in the garden made him feel free.

_____ **2.** In this paragraph, the word **bitter** means

     A. jolly   **C.** steady

     B. angry   **D.** healthy

The skunk has a special way to protect itself. It sprays its enemies with a liquid from under its tail. This liquid has a **foul** smell. So the skunk is left alone.

_____ **3.** In this paragraph, the word **foul** means

     A. great   **C.** cloudy

     B. dandy   **D.** terrible

The leek is a plant like the onion. The people of Wales **respect** the leek. Long ago it helped them fight a war. They could not tell who was on their side. So the people from Wales put leeks in their caps.

_____ **4.** In this paragraph, the word **respect** means

     A. like   **C.** build

     B. melt   **D.** turn

Name_____   **Date** _____

Read the stories. Choose the word or phrase that best completes the sentence.

Catnip is a plant. It belongs to the mint family. It grows wild along many roads. Cats love to roll and play in catnip. They also like to eat it. They like the **taste** of the plant.

_____ **1.** In this paragraph, the word **taste** means
- A. fear
- B. dash
- C. flavor
- D. example

In 1888 there was a terrible **blizzard** in New York City. It lasted for three days. There were strong winds. Blowing snow was all that could be seen. Many people died in this storm.

_____ **2.** In this paragraph, the word **blizzard** means
- A. house
- B. rain
- C. guard
- D. snowstorm

People have **measured** time in many ways. At first, people used the sun, moon, and stars to tell time. Now we use clocks to keep track of time.

_____ **3.** In this paragraph, the word **measured** means
- A. closed
- B. opened
- C. found the length of
- D. put in a bottle

The glass snake is not a snake at all. It is a lizard without legs. Its tail is twice the length of its body. The glass snake can **shed** its tail if it is attacked. A new tail will grow in its place.

_____ **4.** In this paragraph, the word **shed** means
- A. fool
- B. lose
- C. puff up
- D. take in

Name _____   Date _____

Read the stories. Choose the word or phrase that best completes the sentence.

Piranhas are fish. They live in South American rivers. These fish tend to swim in large groups. They will tear the flesh off an animal or person that gets in the water. In just minutes all that is left is the **skeleton**.

_____ **1.** In this paragraph, the word **skeleton** means
    A. key   **C.** butter
    B. pie   **D.** bones

A cartoon is a **humorous** way to tell a story or make a point. A cartoon can be one drawing or a set of drawings. A cartoon may have words with the picture. But words aren't always needed.

_____ **2.** In this paragraph, the word **humorous** means
    A. cozy   **C.** dangerous
    B. funny   **D.** thirsty

Pluto is the planet farthest from the sun. Not much is known about this **distant** planet. It is quite cold there since it is so far from the sun. Scientists don't think that there is any life on Pluto.

_____ **3.** In this paragraph, the word **distant** means
    A. faraway   **C.** lucky
    B. nearby   **D.** pleasant

Long ago, **vessels** crossed the water from northern Europe to other countries. They carried Viking warriors. At first the Vikings fought with people. Then the Vikings decided to trade. They set up many new trade centers.

_____ **4.** In this paragraph, the word **vessels** means
    A. whales   **C.** ships
    B. bottles   **D.** horses

Name_____   Date _____

Read the stories. Choose the word or phrase that best completes the sentence.

Wild flowers grow in many **environments**. Some are found in woods or fields. Others grow on mountains or in streams and ponds. Wild flowers can grow in the desert, too.

_____ **1.** In this paragraph, the word **environments** means
- **A.** blossoms
- **B.** settings
- **C.** oceans
- **D.** insects

Some Americans want to help others. They join the Peace Corps. These workers go to other nations. They try to **educate** the people to help themselves.

_____ **2.** In this paragraph, the word **educate** means
- **A.** present
- **B.** bounce
- **C.** hurry
- **D.** teach

At one time women could not vote or own land. Susan B. Anthony knew that women didn't have the same rights as men. She worked hard to **obtain** equal rights for women. But it was not until many years after her death that women finally won these rights.

_____ **3.** In this paragraph, the word **obtain** means
- **A.** follow
- **B.** notice
- **C.** get
- **D.** move

Sometimes a huge **mass** of ice breaks off from a glacier. It falls into the sea and floats. This block of ice is called an iceberg. Ships must be careful of icebergs.

_____ **4.** In this paragraph, the word **mass** means
- **A.** shade
- **B.** tooth
- **C.** block
- **D.** church

Name_____   Date _____

Read the stories. Choose the phrase that best completes each sentence.

1. Camp Fire is a group that helps young people. Both boys and girls can belong to it. Everyone in the group learns by doing things. Sometimes these young people camp outside and cook dinner over a fire. They also help people. At times they just have fun together. They learn how to share and make friends.

_____ The story mainly tells
  A. when young people have fun
  B. who cooks over a camp fire
  C. how young people learn from Camp Fire
  D. how only girls belong to the group

2. Pet dogs do some things that wild dogs do. Wild dogs eat very quickly. They must eat quickly because the other animals can take their food away. Pet dogs don't usually have this problem, but they still eat quickly. Wild dogs have to make their own beds. So they walk around and around in the grass to make it flat. Pet dogs also turn around a few times before they lie down.

_____ The story mainly tells
  A. who walks around in circles
  B. how pet dogs and wild dogs are alike
  C. how wild dogs make their beds
  D. how pet dogs eat slowly

3. Don't worry if there are times when you get angry. Getting angry can be both good and bad. Many doctors think that it's all right to show your anger sometimes. People who get angry once in a while may live happier lives. But people must be careful when they are angry. Angry people don't always think clearly. They can do things that they'll be sorry about later.

_____ The story mainly tells
  A. why people can't think straight
  B. how people get angry about nothing
  C. how anger can be both good and bad
  D. how anger can make you sick

Go on to the next page.

Name _____   Date _____

Read the stories. Choose the phrase that best completes each sentence.

4. Throw away those skin creams! Doctors say that skin creams don't really help your skin look younger. They say there's a better way to keep your skin looking young. It doesn't cost a penny. Just stay out of the sun during the hottest part of the day. If you must be in the sun, stay out for only a short time. Also, be sure and wear a hat to shade your face.

_____   The story mainly tells

     A. about easy ways to take care of your skin

     B. why skin creams are good for you

     C. how long you should stay out in the sun

     D. how wearing a hat doesn't help

5. We all know that babies make funny sounds. Little by little, babies learn that some sounds will call their mother and father. Other sounds will get them food. Yet some sounds will bring them nothing at all. Babies learn to talk by finding out which sounds work best.

_____   The story mainly tells

     A. which babies make the loudest noises

     B. why a baby's first sounds are important

     C. when babies first start to make noise

     D. how babies aren't smart

6. It's harder walking in space than it is walking on Earth. When the first men landed on the moon, they had trouble walking. So space scientists decided to study other creatures to learn how they walk. Spiders are good walking machines. Scientists watched spiders very closely. Then they tried making a machine that would walk as well as the spider. This machine will be used to explore space.

_____   The story mainly tells

     A. why spiders walk like machines

     B. how the new machines walk

     C. how the spider is a model for a walking machine

     D. how the men walked on a star

Name_____   Date _____

Read the stories. Choose the phrase that best completes each sentence.

1. The mind can work very well for many years. People used to think that age slowed down the mind. But this isn't true. The mind is just like any other muscle in the body. The more you use it, the stronger it becomes. Muscles that aren't used will grow weak. Muscles that are used will stay strong. Older people who use their minds will think as well as ever.

_____   The story mainly tells
   A. how using the mind keeps it strong
   B. who has the biggest muscles in their arms
   C. who is smarter than other people
   D. how the mind becomes weak with age

2. Horse shows are the place to see beautiful horses. The riders and horses get scores for each event. First all the riders walk their horses around the ring. Then they trot the horses, making them go faster and faster. Finally they gallop. When they jump over logs or ponds, the riders must not fall. The best riders and horses get ribbons and prizes.

_____   The story mainly tells
   A. which kinds of horses jump the highest
   B. who gets prizes for galloping
   C. what horses and riders do in horse shows
   D. how the horses jump fences

3. Many people are afraid of flying in airplanes. Sometimes they're so afraid that they get sick. This is a problem. These people can never visit friends who live far away. Doctors have started classes that teach people about planes. The people practice flying in planes. It works, too. Many people have learned to get over their fear of flying!

_____   The story mainly tells
   A. why people are afraid of the dark
   B. how people learn to get over their fear of flying
   C. why people are afraid of flying
   D. how these people learn to fly airplanes

Name_____   Date _____

Read the stories. Choose the phrase that best completes each sentence.

1. Some butterflies lay their eggs on just one kind of plant. By tasting the plant, they know which one is right. Sometimes butterflies taste the wrong plant. So they fly to another plant and taste again. When they find the right plant, they lay their eggs there. Soon the eggs hatch. The hungry babies eat the plant their mother chose!

_____   The story mainly tells
    A. when baby butterflies come out of eggs
    B. how butterflies choose where to lay eggs
    C. what flies from one plant to another
    D. how butterflies always taste the right plant

2. Kings and queens had the earliest zoos. They wanted to show off their money by keeping strange animals. Later, people kept animals in zoos because they wanted to learn about them. Students could take classes at the zoo. Today, zoos try to help certain animals. These animals are disappearing from their wild homes. So zoos help keep these animals safe.

_____   The story mainly tells
    A. how rulers showed off their money
    B. which people learned about zoo animals
    C. how zoos have changed over the years
    D. how animals will never disappear

3. Years ago doctors made house calls. They took care of sick people at home. Later they stopped making house calls. They wanted people to go to hospitals instead. But hospitals cost so much money. Now some doctors have decided that the old way is better. They have found that house calls cost people less than going to the hospital.

_____   The story mainly tells
    A. which sick people go to hospitals
    B. why some doctors now go to people's houses
    C. when doctors changed their minds
    D. how much money doctors make today

Name_____   Date _____

Read the stories. Choose the phrase that best completes each sentence.

1. The first dollhouses were built for grown-ups. These houses were as tall as people. They were filled with pretty things. Rich people made these dollhouses look like their own homes. Only later did they build smaller dollhouses for children. Some of these are still around. They help us learn what real houses looked like long ago.

_____ The story mainly tells
- A. when people made dollhouses for children
- B. which dollhouses were the tallest
- C. what the first dollhouses were like
- D. which people didn't build dollhouses

2. Mother ducks take baby ducks away from each other. This is the way it happens. The mother ducks take their babies swimming. Soon the pond is full of ducks. The mother ducks quack. They swim around the baby ducks. The mother duck that quacks loudest gets the greatest number of babies. Some mother ducks may have forty baby ducks. Others may have only two or three.

_____ The story mainly tells
- A. which duck quacks the loudest
- B. how mother ducks take babies away
- C. when the ducks go swimming
- D. how baby ducks choose their mother

3. The African American man stared at the picture on the wall. It was a very old family picture. The man in the picture was a soldier. He died for his country. The eyes of the man in the picture seemed to ask, "Remember me?" But the young man thought, "No. People don't remember you." So he quit his job. He worked at passing a law that would put up a statue in Washington, D.C. The statue would honor the five thousand African Americans who died in the War for Independence.

_____ The story mainly tells
- A. in which war the man in the picture died
- B. about a statue for African Americans
- C. who fought for our country's independence
- D. that the statue honors only white men

Name_____   Date _____

Read the stories. Choose the phrase that best completes each sentence.

1. Police use fingerprints to tell one person from another. Roses have fingerprints, too. But the prints aren't found on the pretty flowers. They're on the leaves. Each rose leaf has holes in it. The holes are like people's fingerprints. The holes of each different kind of rose have a special shape and size. By looking at the holes, people can tell the name of the rose.

_____ The story mainly tells

   A. what the holes in flowers are like
   B. why flowers have fingerprints
   C. how rose leaves have fingerprints
   D. how all of the holes are the same size

2. Many families in Japan collect dolls. These families have a Doll Day for Girls and a Doll Day for Boys. On the girls' day, families bring out special dolls. The dolls are dressed as old kings and queens from Japan. On the boys' day, families bring out other dolls. The dolls are dressed as famous fighters from the past. These doll days are very special to the people of Japan.

_____ The story mainly tells

   A. who plays with dolls in Japan
   B. which dolls are famous in Japan
   C. what doll days are like in Japan
   D. how much the famous dolls cost

3. Calamity Jane was a famous woman of the Wild West. She was famous because she was so tough. She lived during the 1800s. She learned to ride a horse and shoot a gun at an early age. People could always hear her coming. She also liked dressing in men's clothes. There weren't many women like Calamity Jane.

_____ The story mainly tells

   A. why Calamity Jane was famous
   B. how Calamity Jane dressed
   C. when Calamity Jane rode a horse
   D. when Calamity Jane was called a coward

Name _____   Date _____

Read the stories. Choose the phrase that best completes each sentence.

1. Children learn their first lessons in banking when they use piggy banks. Children put pennies in their banks and wait for the number of pennies to grow. The money is safe there. When the bank is full, the child can buy something with the money. In the same way, children's parents put their money in a real bank. It's safe there. They can add more money every month. Later they can use it to buy the things they need.

_____ The story mainly tells

     A. how children spend their money

     B. how a piggy bank is a lesson in banking

     C. when grown people put money in a bank

     D. why grown people don't use piggy banks

2. Zoo elephants get very good care. Each morning zookeepers give them a special bath. They wash the elephants with water and a brush. Then they paint oil on their skin and rub oil on their feet. This is very important in elephant care. It helps the elephants feel good. When zoo visitors come to see them, the elephants are happy.

_____ The story mainly tells

     A. why zookeepers have happy lives

     B. who paints oil on elephants

     C. why zookeepers give elephants special care

     D. how much elephants eat

3. Not long ago, people raised their own chickens. They fed the chickens leftover food. They also gathered fresh eggs every day. Every morning the roosters awakened everybody. Sometimes the family cooked a chicken for dinner. Today life has changed. Most people buy chickens and eggs at stores. They have clocks to awaken them.

_____ The story mainly tells

     A. why people once raised chickens

     B. why chickens give fresh eggs

     C. when the family cooked a chicken

     D. where the chicken pens were found

Name _____   Date _____

Read the stories. Choose the phrase that best completes each sentence.

1. Scientists use balloons to study the weather. They hook machines to balloons and send them up in the sky. The balloons rise in the sky until they finally pop. When this happens the machines fall to earth. Then scientists take these machines back to the lab to learn more about the weather.

_____   The story mainly tells

A. about a machine that helps in the study of weather

B. why scientists like to fly balloons

C. how far the machines go up into the air

D. how quickly the balloons pop

2. All winter long bears do nothing but sleep. To get ready for their winter sleep, they eat. They eat much food to get fat. The fat will become food their bodies will use while they sleep. Bears choose sleeping places such as caves. But they might also choose a hollow log or even a big pile of brush. If it gets warm on a winter day, the bear might come out to walk around. But it doesn't stay out long. Only in the spring do they finally get up and look for food.

_____   The story mainly tells

A. what kind of life a bear leads

B. who likes caves for sleeping

C. where bears sleep in the summer

D. why bears love honey

3. Many farmers today grow fields of yellow sunflowers. People have many uses for sunflower seeds. After the seeds are dried and salted, people buy them to eat. Some sunflower seeds are pressed to make cooking oil. Some seeds are also ground to make a kind of butter.

_____   The story mainly tells

A. why people eat salty seeds

B. how sunflower seeds are of great value

C. who uses cooking oil

D. who likes sunflower butter

Name_____   Date _____

Read the stories. Choose the phrase that best completes each sentence.

1. Long ago Jane Addams didn't believe that poor people were treated fairly. She wanted a law that would keep poor children from having to work. She also thought that poor women shouldn't have to work more than eight hours a day. Many of her wishes became laws.

_____   The story mainly tells
   A. how Jane Addams worked to help the poor
   B. why people are poor
   C. when children should work long hours
   D. how poor people were treated fairly

2. Everyone knows the kind of ham people eat. But another ham is the person who runs a radio station for fun. Hams use radios to talk to other hams, even in other countries. What happens if two hams don't speak the same language? Hams have made a new language that all hams learn. It's called the Q signal language because everything starts with a *Q*. For instance, *QTH?* means "Where are you?"

_____   The story mainly tells
   A. about a new language for hams everywhere
   B. who listens to radios
   C. about different kinds of meat
   D. how radio hams like to eat ham

3. Everything is made up of tiny things called atoms. How small are atoms? Take out a pencil. Make a tiny dot on this page. Now sharpen your pencil. Make an even smaller dot on the page. The tiniest dot that you could make would be made of millions of atoms. That's how small atoms are!

_____   The story mainly tells
   A. that atoms are so small we can't even see them
   B. where to put a dot
   C. what a pencil is made of
   D. how an atom is bigger than a dot

Name_____   Date _____

Read the stories. Choose the phrase that best completes each sentence.

1. Katherine Anne Porter was born in Texas in 1890. She did not go to college, but she read many books. Porter wrote stories. But people wanted her to write a book. Her first book took twenty years to write. It was *Ship of Fools*. It was a big seller. Later it was made into a movie.

_____   The story mainly tells

    A. about Porter's first book

    B. that Porter was a Texan

    C. that Porter liked to go to the movies

    D. that Porter wrote many books

2. Neil Armstrong was an astronaut. In 1969 he did something no one else had done before. He set foot on the moon. He said, "That's one small step for a man, one giant leap for mankind." Edwin Aldrin followed Armstrong. They placed an American flag on the moon.

_____   The story mainly tells
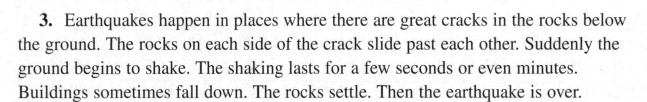

    A. what Neil Armstrong said on the moon

    B. who first walked on the moon

    C. how Armstrong and Aldrin reached the moon

    D. what clothing Armstrong wore on the moon

3. Earthquakes happen in places where there are great cracks in the rocks below the ground. The rocks on each side of the crack slide past each other. Suddenly the ground begins to shake. The shaking lasts for a few seconds or even minutes. Buildings sometimes fall down. The rocks settle. Then the earthquake is over.

_____   The story mainly tells

    A. what happens during an earthquake

    B. about the San Francisco earthquake

    C. what to do during an earthquake

    D. how to stop an earthquake

Name _____   Date _____

Read the stories. Choose the phrase that best completes each sentence.

1. Two things make a tree a conifer. It must make seeds in its cones. It must also have needlelike leaves. Conifers are called evergreen trees. They look green all the time. Conifers lose and replace their leaves. But they never lose all their leaves at the same time.

_____   This story mainly tells
   A. another name for the evergreen tree
   B. about conifer trees
   C. about different types of conifer trees
   D. when conifer trees lose their leaves

2. This book is read by sight. Braille is read by touch. Braille letters are made up of raised dots. People who are blind read by running their fingers over the letters. Braille was named after the man who invented it. Louis Braille invented Braille in 1829.

_____   This story mainly tells
   A. how Louis Braille invented Braille
   B. how to read Braille
   C. about a special kind of writing for the blind
   D. how to read this book

3. Hair has color because it contains melanin. Dark hair has much melanin in it. Light hair has less. As people grow older, their hair has less melanin. But the hair keeps growing. So the hair looks gray or white because it doesn't have any melanin.

_____   This story mainly tells
   A. how hair grows
   B. how to change the color of hair
   C. where melanin comes from
   D. why hair is light or dark

Name _____   Date _____

Read the stories. Choose the phrase that best completes each sentence.

---

1. A set is the place in which a movie is filmed. Carpenters build sets to show scenes where the action takes place. Some sets are painted to look like real rooms. They can be used for plays, films, or television shows. Sets can also be built to look like the outdoors. A set for a whole street or town can even be built.

_____   The story mainly tells

    A. how television shows and movies are made

    B. that films are made outdoors

    C. how sets are used

    D. that carpenters build sets

---

2. There are many Greek legends. One tells the story of Icarus, a man in prison. His father made wings of wax and feathers for him. Icarus attached the wings to his arms and was able to escape from the prison. He flew over the sea like a bird. But Icarus flew too close to the sun. The sun melted his wax wings, and Icarus fell to his death.

_____   The story mainly tells

    A. about the Greek legend of Icarus

    B. about many Greek legends

    C. about making wings of wax

    D. why Icarus was in prison

---

3. When Ethel Waters was a child, she was poor. She worked as a maid for five dollars a day. Ethel knew she was talented. She began singing. She worked very hard. She sang and acted in movies and plays. In 1950 Ethel Waters won an award for acting in a play. She became known as the actress with the golden voice.

_____   The story mainly tells

    A. that Ethel Waters was poor

    B. where Ethel Waters grew up

    C. about a famous maid

    D. how Ethel Waters became famous

Name_____   Date _____

Read the stories. Choose the phrase that best completes each sentence.

1.   Henry González wanted to run for the Texas legislature. He went to political leaders for help. They said that a Mexican American could not win. But he ran anyway. He spent $300 on his campaign. The other men who ran spent much more money. González lost the election. But he lost by only a few votes. Then González ran for city council and won. He went on to win other state and national offices.

_____   The story mainly tells

    A. about a man who became a political leader

    B. that González lived in Texas

    C. about González's high-priced campaign

    D. how political leaders helped González

2.   Dixy Lee Ray wanted to become governor. People laughed at her. There had been only four women governors in the United States. All had been elected with the help of their husbands. But Ray had never been married. She ran for governor on her own. Ray became the first woman governor of Washington.

_____   The story mainly tells

    A. about the first woman governor in the United States

    B. why Dixy Lee Ray wanted to become governor

    C. about a woman who ran her own campaign

    D. who Dixy Lee Ray's husband was

3.   When an io moth is resting, its wings are folded. If the moth sees a hungry bird, it unfolds its wings. The wings have markings called eyespots. Each spot looks like a big eye. The eyespots scare the bird away.

_____   The story mainly tells

    A. which animals have eyespots

    B. about the size of eyespots

    C. how an io moth protects itself

    D. about the color of an io moth

Name _____ Date _____

Read the stories. Choose the phrase that best completes each sentence.

1. Marina López was sick. Her doctors said that walking would be good for her health. She and her husband began playing golf. Their daughter, Nancy, would go with them to the golf course. They noticed that she could hit the ball long distances. Nancy won a golf tournament when she was nine years old. By the time she was 12, she had won a state women's tournament. Nancy became a professional golfer when she was 19. Nancy López is now in the golfer's hall of fame.

_____ The story mainly tells

    A. how many tournaments Nancy López has won

    B. how Marina López's health improved

    C. how Nancy López started playing golf

    D. that Nancy López's mother was a famous golfer

2. King Louis XIV of France was a short man. He wanted to look taller. So he ordered high heels for his shoes. Then he had his shoes trimmed with lace, bows, and jewels. One pair of shoes had bows that were 16 inches wide. He had artists paint scenes on the heels of his shoes. Soon other men in France wore high-heeled shoes with flowers and bows.

_____ The story mainly tells

    A. why high-heeled shoes were invented

    B. how tall King Louis XIV was

    C. how the king painted his heels

    D. about shoes that men wear today

3. The Loch Ness Monster has been seen many times. It lives in a lake in Scotland called Loch Ness. The waters of Loch Ness are the color of coffee. So no one has been able to take a clear picture of the monster or catch it. The monster is said to be about twenty feet long. It has a tiny head and a long neck. Its big body has flippers and many humps.

_____ The story mainly tells

    A. that the monster does not exist

    B. how many people have seen the monster

    C. where Loch Ness is located

    D. how no one has proved that the monster is real

Name _____   Date _____

Read the stories. Choose the phrase that best completes each sentence.

1. Jay and Jean went to the store to buy toys for their baby. "Let's get a toy cat that has painted eyes," said Jay. "Button eyes can fall off, and the baby might eat them." They also wanted a wooden train set. Jean made sure that the train didn't have any sharp edges. They also bought a set of paints. The paints were marked *Safe for all ages*. Jay and Jean knew that their baby would like these toys.

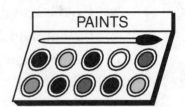

_____   From this story you can tell that
      A. Jean was a painting teacher
      B. Jean liked the train set the best
      C. Jean and Jay bought only safe toys
      D. Jean wanted a train with sharp edges

2. People are always thinking of new things to sell in machines. Most machines sell candy and drinks. But now machines even sell flowers. Machines are placed where many people will see them. For instance, lunchrooms are a good place to put candy machines. Baseball parks are a good place for drink machines.

_____   From this story you can tell that
      A. drinks from a machine taste best
      B. some machines sell things besides food
      C. all drink machines are found in baseball parks
      D. machines are placed where people won't see them

3. Carla woke up when the rooster crowed. She lit a candle. Then she built a fire in the fireplace. The fire would help her make a good, warm breakfast. When Juan woke up, Carla sent him to gather more firewood. Juan also brought water from the well. After he ate, Juan walked the horses to the field to plow.

_____   From this story you can tell that
      A. Carla and Juan have many cows
      B. Carla and Juan have six children
      C. Carla and Juan probably live on a farm
      D. Carla and Juan plow the fields together

Go on to the next page.

Name _____   Date _____

Read the stories. Choose the phrase that best completes each sentence.

4. The shaggy, little animal went up to the back door. It rattled the screen door with its front paw and then sat down. It was quiet for a while. But soon a face appeared at the door, and then there was a scream of joy. "It's Goldie!" a girl's voice said. "She's come back."

_____   From this story you can tell that
           A. Goldie had lived at this house at one time
           B. the animal had never seen this house before
           C. the girl didn't know why the animal was there
           D. Goldie must be a dog

5. In the morning Becky came downstairs. "I don't like this house at all," the girl told her parents. "It smells funny." Her mother asked if she had seen the wild strawberries growing in the front yard. Her father mentioned the pony he had seen at the neighboring house. The girl's eyes lit up.

_____   You can conclude that this family
           A. is about to move to a new house
           B. has just moved into this house
           C. will leave the house because of Becky's feelings
           D. will punish Becky for being rude

6. The man tried to balance himself, but he wobbled. The wheels seemed to go in every direction at once. When he hit a bump, his foot lost its grip on the pedal. He put his feet on the ground. Then he let go of the handlebars and sat straight up on the narrow seat with his arms forward. "I haven't done this in a long time," he said with a laugh.

_____   You can tell that the man is
           A. driving a car for the first time in a long time
           B. trying to use a mixer in the kitchen
           C. trying to ride a tricycle
           D. trying to ride a bicycle

Name_____   Date _____

Read the stories. Choose the phrase that best completes each sentence.

1. Baseball is a big sport in Japan. The rules are the same as those in America. But the customs are different. Players in Japan don't show their anger when they're *out*. They don't try to hurt the player from the other team as the player slides into second base. Also, when the fans clap, the players bow to them.

_____   From this story you can tell that
      A. Japanese players do not slide into second base
      B. American players show their anger
      C. Japanese players can play better
      D. Japanese players wave when the fans clap

2. The knight in chess is different from the other pieces. The knight is the only piece that can jump over the other ones. This move comes from the days of the knights. Knights traveled far and in search of adventure. They traveled off the regular road. There they often met enemies to fight. The knight in chess also does not have a regular move. The knight's move in chess is like the life of the knight of long ago.

_____   From this story you can tell that
      A. all chess pieces move in the same way
      B. the knight in chess has a regular move
      C. chess pieces move in different ways
      D. the knight in chess does not move

3. Long ago Spanish ships sailed to America. They landed in a warm part of the country. The sun shone brightly there. Flowers bloomed even in the winter. There wasn't any snow. The Spanish people called the land Florida. It is the Spanish word for "blooming." That's how the state got its name.

_____   From this story you can tell that
      A. American states can have Spanish names
      B. the Spanish people came in the spring
      C. *Florida* means "snow" in Spanish
      D. the Spanish ships landed in Texas

Name _____   Date _____

Read the stories. Choose the phrase that best completes each sentence.

1. Sid paid his fare and found a seat. He looked out the window as they passed street after street. When a woman with a baby got on, he got up and gave her his seat. He was glad that his ride was short.

_____ **1.** You can tell that Sid is
   A. on a plane
   B. in a taxi
   C. on a bus
   D. on a boat

2. Fran marked her place and then closed the book. She put it on the table next to her bed. Then she fluffed up the pillow and set the alarm clock. She checked the window to make sure it was open. Then she crawled under the covers and fell asleep.

_____ You can conclude that Fran
   A. finished reading her book
   B. wanted some fresh air in the room
   C. works in an office
   D. leaves the porch light on at night

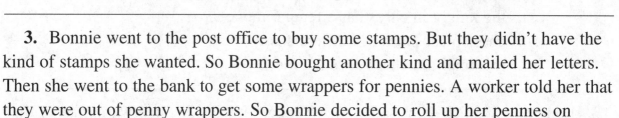

3. Bonnie went to the post office to buy some stamps. But they didn't have the kind of stamps she wanted. So Bonnie bought another kind and mailed her letters. Then she went to the bank to get some wrappers for pennies. A worker told her that they were out of penny wrappers. So Bonnie decided to roll up her pennies on another day.

_____ Bonnie's two errands were alike because
   A. she walked to both places
   B. she bought something in both places
   C. she used pennies in both places
   D. neither place had what she wanted

Name_____   Date _____

Read the stories. Choose the phrase that best completes each sentence.

1. Most desert plants have sharp stickers. These spines help the desert plant drink water. Morning mist also forms big drops on these stickers. Then the drops fall, and the plant drinks the water. The spines also make the hot desert winds circle around the plant. This keeps the wind from taking the plant's water.

_____ From this story you can tell that
  A. most desert plants need spines to live
  B. the spines on desert plants do not help them
  C. desert plants do not live very long
  D. the wind does not blow in the desert

2. The War of 1812 was a strange war. It started when British ships stopped some American ships. The angry Americans warned the British to be careful. The British agreed to stop making so much trouble. But there were no telephones at that time. So the news didn't get to America very quickly. Just two days after the British agreed to stop causing trouble, the Americans started the war.

_____ From this story you can tell that
  A. telephones might have kept the war from starting
  B. the Americans liked fighting wars back then
  C. the Americans did not have very many ships
  D. the Americans never warned the British

3. "Don't jump!" the fire fighters shouted. The woman stood at a window on the eleventh floor. The fire burned behind her. She was very scared. The fire fighters climbed to the twelfth floor. One of them found an old hose in the hallway. "Tie this to me," he said. "I'll climb out the window. She'll see that we're near, and maybe she won't jump." Because of this the woman's life was saved.

_____ From this story you can tell that
  A. the fire was on the twelfth floor of the building
  B. the jump would have killed the woman
  C. the woman had to go to the hospital
  D. the woman wasn't scared at all

Name_____   Date _____

Read the stories. Choose the phrase that best completes each sentence.

1. Wilbur Voliva believed that the earth was flat. He said that the sun was only three thousand miles away. He didn't believe that the sun was millions of miles away. In fact, Voliva didn't believe anything that scientists said. He also wanted to prove them wrong. So each year Voliva offered a big money prize. It was for anyone who could prove him wrong and show that the world was round.

_____   From this story you can tell that
    A. Voliva thought that the earth was round
    B. scientists thought that the sun was millions of miles away
    C. Voliva believed everything that scientists said
    D. Voliva knew much about the sun

2. Dan and Lola are married to each other. Both of them are truck drivers. They like driving trucks. They think that most truck drivers are fine people. But they also think that today truck drivers have a bad name. So Dan and Lola are working to get some laws passed. These laws would make truck drivers who drive too fast stay off the road.

_____   From this story you can tell that
    A. many truck drivers are married to each other
    B. some truck drivers today drive too fast
    C. most truck drivers carry food to other places
    D. most truck drivers are bad people

3. The town was on fire. Jim Root was the train engineer. He knew that the fire would burn the station and all the people on the train! So he started the train to get it out of town. But the worst part of the fire lay in front of him. So he drove the train backwards the whole way. Finally the train reached a lake outside of town. Root had saved everybody's life!

_____   From this story you can tell that
    A. the last car on the train burned up
    B. Jim had never driven a train before
    C. the train could not be turned around
    D. the lake was near the train station

Name_____   Date _____

Read the stories. Choose the phrase that best completes each sentence.

1. The plant with the biggest seed in the world is called the coconut of the sea. Its huge seed can grow to be as big as a beach ball. It can weigh as much as fifty pounds.

_____   From this story you can tell that
A. this plant probably grows in the United States
B. this seed wouldn't make a good beach ball
C. the seed is the size of a big orange
D. the seed tastes like coconut

2. Let's say that you wanted to write down all the words while someone was talking. It would be very hard. People talk much faster than they write. But you could learn a special kind of writing. It's called shorthand. Shorthand doesn't look at all like the writing in this book. For instance, a straight line stands for am. So you'd have to learn to read shorthand, too.

_____   From this story you can tell that
A. today many people are learning shorthand
B. shorthand is very easy to learn
C. the word *the* looks different in shorthand
D. people talk slower than they write

3. Nellie Bly worked for a newspaper. She managed to report stories that nobody else could. Once she wanted to know how doctors treated the poor people. So she dressed in rags and pretended to be sick. She told them that she didn't have any money. She was taken to a hospital for the poor. There she had to sleep on the floor and eat terrible food. Later Nellie Bly wrote a story about her stay at this hospital. Her story surprised many people.

_____   From this story you can tell that
A. some hospitals were not kind to the poor
B. Bly got sick when she was in the hospital
C. Bly won a prize for writing the story
D. the food at the hospital for the poor was good

Name_____   Date _____

Read the stories. Choose the phrase that best completes each sentence.

1. Did you know you can start a campfire with ice? First find a large piece of very clear ice. Then melt it down in the palms of your hands. When it is ready, the ice should look like a lens. It should have smooth curves on both sides. Finally use the ice to direct the sun's rays onto paper or wood shavings. This will start the fire.

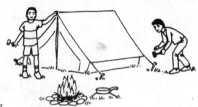

_____ The story suggests that
   A. ice burns
   B. the ice will freeze the fire
   C. the warmth of your hands melts the ice
   D. the ice should be curved on one side only

2. Nat Love was a special breed of man. He was a restless cowboy who helped settle the Wild West. As a young man, Love was a slave in Tennessee. Set free by the Civil War, Love learned to herd cattle and to use a gun. In Deadwood, South Dakota, Nat won a big cowboy contest. There he gained his nickname, Deadwood Dick.

_____ You can tell from the story that Nat Love
   A. drove a fast car
   B. was a slave all his life
   C. grew up in Texas
   D. was a skilled cowboy

3. Most whales survive by eating small sea creatures known as krill. Some companies were planning to harvest krill. Mary Cahoon and Mary McWhinnie were afraid that this harvest would cause whales to starve. They went to the South Pole to study the problem. They were the first women to spend a whole winter at the cold South Pole.

_____ The story suggests that the companies
   A. planned to harvest wheat
   B. weren't worried about whales
   C. liked warm weather
   D. went ice-skating often

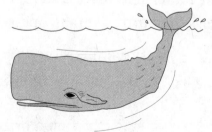

Name _____   Date _____

Read the stories. Choose the phrase that best completes each sentence.

1. Today many men wear beards. But men have been shaving off their beards for thousands of years. At first the beard stood for manhood. Men shaved so that they could offer their beards to the gods. This was a sign of their obedience to the gods. The ancient soldiers were ordered not to wear beards. The beards could be grabbed very easily by enemy soldiers!

_____   From the story you <u>cannot</u> tell
      A. whether or not men still wear beards today
      B. what the beard was a sign of at one time
      C. why men shaved their beards long ago
      D. whether or not soldiers today can wear beards

2. When Tony woke up, he looked out the window. What luck! The mountain was covered with snow. Quickly he pulled on his long underwear and other warm clothes. He ate a good, hot breakfast so that he'd have plenty of energy. Then he checked his equipment. He clomped in his heavy boots toward the door and looked at the slopes.

_____   In this story the mood is
      A. angry
      B. dangerous
      C. happy
      D. silly

3. Nina was walking down a long hall. She kept turning corners and looking for a certain door. But all the doors she found were the wrong ones. Suddenly a bell rang, and Nina thought, "Oh, I must run or I'll be late." But the bell kept ringing, and Nina couldn't run. Instead, she opened her eyes. The telephone beside her bed was ringing loudly.

_____   From the story you can tell that
      A. the telephone awoke Nina from her dream
      B. Nina was in school
      C. Nina didn't want to answer the telephone
      D. Nina was glad the telephone rang

Name _____   Date _____

Read the stories. Choose the phrase that best completes each sentence.

1. Do you cover your mouth when you yawn? Today we think of this act as a part of good manners. But the early Romans covered their yawns out of fear. They thought that their souls might escape during a yawn. They believed that a hand to the lips kept them alive.

_____   From the story you can tell that

    A. the Romans thought yawning caused death

    B. your teeth might fall out if you yawn

    C. yawns are bad for your health

    D. the Romans slept much of the time

2. Valentina Tereshkova was nervous. She knew she'd soon make history. It was a still morning in 1963. She sat strapped in her seat. At last the Soviet spaceship began to shake. Its great engines roared. The ship climbed from the launch pad. It built up speed. Soon it was racing through the sky. Within minutes Valentina had become the first woman in space.

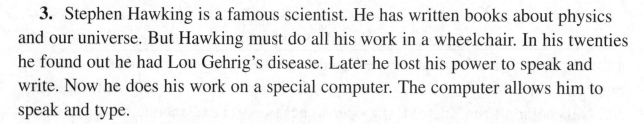

_____   The story does <u>not</u> tell

    A. when Tereshkova made her flight

    B. how Tereshkova gained fame

    C. how long it took Tereshkova to become famous

    D. how many people went with Tereshkova

3. Stephen Hawking is a famous scientist. He has written books about physics and our universe. But Hawking must do all his work in a wheelchair. In his twenties he found out he had Lou Gehrig's disease. Later he lost his power to speak and write. Now he does his work on a special computer. The computer allows him to speak and type.

_____   The story suggests that Stephen Hawking

    A. is a baseball player

    B. uses a computer to walk

    C. can't use a regular typewriter

    D. likes to play video games

Name _____   Date _____

Read the stories. Choose the phrase that best completes each sentence.

1. Karen could not walk or dance. But she loved to move in her wheelchair while she listened to music. Her favorite singer was Elvis Presley. One day she decided she would become his pen pal. She wrote a letter to Elvis and mailed it. Days went by, and no reply came. At first Karen feared that Elvis might not write. But she kept hoping. At last the special letter came. It was the first of many.

_____   The story suggests that Karen
     A. did not know how to write
     B. lost her letter at the post office
     C. became a pen pal with Elvis
     D. lost all her hope

2. Don't you wish you could break free of Earth's gravity? Then you could float in space. Spaceships have to break free of Earth's gravity to reach space. They must go very fast. In fact, they must travel at seven miles per second to break Earth's pull. That is about twenty-five thousand miles per hour.

_____   The story does <u>not</u> tell
     A. how fast spaceships must go to reach space
     B. what happens if a spaceship goes too slowly
     C. that spaceships break free of Earth's pull
     D. that you could float in space

3. As a lawyer Thurgood Marshall worked in many civil rights trials. He believed in "equal justice under the law." Marshall tried hard to gain that goal. He won many cases. He helped win equal rights for all Americans. Marshall's hard work paid off. First he was made a judge. Then he was picked to serve on the highest court in the land. He was made a Supreme Court justice. He became the first African American to hold that post.

_____   You can tell from the story that Marshall
     A. was never a judge
     B. did not work hard as a lawyer
     C. mainly worked in traffic court
     D. believed in equal rights for all

77

Name_____   Date _____

Read the stories. Choose the phrase that best completes each sentence.

1. A ship's speed was once figured by using a log. A log was thrown overboard at the front of the boat. Then time was kept until the log passed the stern, or rear. The length of the ship was known. So the captain would know how long the ship took to travel its length. The speed would be written in a *logbook*. That name is still used for the diary of a ship.

_____   The story does <u>not</u> tell
        A. what kind of tree the log came from
        B. how a ship's speed was once figured
        C. what the captain would write the speed in
        D. where the log was thrown overboard

2. For years traveling farm workers were not treated well. At last César Chávez could stand no more. He thought farm workers should be paid more. He wanted better working conditions for them. To gain these he formed a union. The group went on strike against grape growers in 1965. The strike lasted for five years. But finally their demands were met.

_____   The story suggests that César Chávez
        A. thought farm workers were paid too much
        B. grew tired of the bad treatment of farm workers
        C. worked in rice fields
        D. did not win the strike

3. In 1814 much of Washington, D.C., was burned by the British. They burned the President's home, too. But Americans rebuilt the capital. The burned boards of the President's home were painted a bright white. Since then the mansion has been known as the White House.

_____   You can tell from the story
        A. that the White House was once blue
        B. how long the city took to rebuild
        C. why the British burned the city
        D. how the White House got its name

Name_____   Date _____

Read the stories. Choose the phrase that best completes each sentence.

1. Francis Marion was a small, thin man. But he became a hero of the American Revolution. He set up his base in a South Carolina swamp. From there his soldiers launched raids on British camps. They caused the British troops all sorts of trouble. Marion's plans were always sly. Because of this he became known as the Swamp Fox.

_____   From the story you can tell
        A. when the American Revolution was fought
        B. that Francis Marion tricked British troops
        C. that Francis Marion was captured
        D. how many British camps Marion's men raided

2. Tooth care has always been important. The oldest known tooth care product was a "chew stick." It was used in Egypt five thousand years ago. This stick was rubbed on the teeth to clean them. Today's toothbrush has bristles. This type of brush was first used in China around A.D. 1500. Hog bristles were used at first. Now nylon bristles are used.

_____   The story suggests that
        A. nylon bristles were first used around A.D. 1500
        B. hog bristles are mostly used now
        C. most people never use toothbrushes
        D. the chew stick did not have bristles

3. The Aztecs lived in ancient Mexico. They believed that their god had four sons. When one son would try to rule the earth, the others would fight him. So life on Earth was destroyed four times. At last, in the fifth age, the brothers agreed to rule together.

_____   You can tell from the story that
        A. the four brothers fought often
        B. the brothers were always friendly
        C. none of the brothers wanted to rule the earth
        D. the brothers finally agreed in the fourth age

Name _____ Date _____

Read the stories. Choose the phrase that best completes each sentence.

1. Scientists know that our universe is very old. Most think it is about 15 billion years old. Suppose that all that time added up to one year. This would mean that the dinosaurs lived in mid-December. Humans would have been on earth for a few minutes. Also, your life would be just two seconds long!

_____ The story suggests that the human race is
A. older than the universe
B. much younger than the universe
C. older than the dinosaurs
D. only two weeks old

2. In Navajo legends the first ones on Earth were First Man, First Woman, and Coyote. They lived in the first world and then in the second world. Later they moved to the third world. A water monster lived in the third world. Coyote stole two of the monster's children. The monster grew angry and caused the water to rise. First Man, First Woman, and Coyote then had to escape to the fourth world.

_____ You <u>cannot</u> tell from the story
A. who the first ones on Earth were
B. in which world the water monster lived
C. who caused the water to rise
D. why Coyote stole the water monster's children

3. Stars do not last forever. After billions of years they just burn out. Some stars suddenly brighten before they dim. These stars are called novas. *Nova* means "new" in Latin. The novas seem to be new stars. The last great nova was in 1054. It could be seen even in the daytime. It outshone everything in the sky except the sun and moon.

_____ You can tell from the story that
A. novas are not seen very often
B. great novas happen all the time
C. all stars become novas
D. the nova of 1054 was not very bright

Name_____   Date _____

Read the stories. Choose the sentence that best answers each question.

1. The village people chose a boy to guard the sheep. It was an important job.
If a wolf came near, the boy was supposed to call the people in the village. Then they
would come to help him. The boy watched the sheep for a little while. Then he decided
to have some fun. He cried out loudly, "Wolf! Wolf!" The people rushed out to fight
the wolf. When they arrived the boy was laughing at them. There was no wolf.

_____   Which of these sentences is probably true?

A. Everyone thought the joke was funny.

B. Several of the sheep got lost.

C. The people were angry at the boy.

D. The boy was very kind.

2. In the 1950s golf was a new sport in Japan. Many people liked the game. The
golfers practiced and practiced. They tried to hit the small, hard balls across the golf
course grass. But those who played golf were in great danger. In fact, people on the
golf course had to wear hard hats for their own safety.

_____   Which of these sentences is probably true?

A. Playing golf in the United States is not very safe.

B. At first the golfers in Japan didn't play very well.

C. People in Japan also played football.

D. Golfers in Japan were often hit by lightning.

3. The young donkey stopped in the middle of the road. Ted and Sally jumped
down from their cart and looked at the brown animal. First Ted yelled at the donkey,
but it would not move. Then Sally tapped it with a stick, but still nothing happened.
Ted even used a carrot to make the donkey go on, but it would not. Giving up, Ted
and Sally sat down by the road to wait.

_____   Which of these sentences is probably true?

A. The road was bumpy and full of holes.

B. The donkey wouldn't give in easily.

C. Ted and Sally were old and tired.

D. The donkey was very hungry.

Go on to the next page.

Name_____   Date _____

Read the stories. Mark whether each statement is an inference or a fact.

4. Shoes were not always made differently for right and left feet. For hundreds of years, shoemakers made shoes to fit either foot. After shoes were worn for a while, the leather would stretch to fit the right or left foot. Around 1850 special sewing machines made it easier to produce shoes. Several years after that, shoes were made for each foot.

Fact Inference

○   ○   **A.** Shoes stretched to fit each foot.

○   ○   **B.** Shoes were made of stretchy material.

○   ○   **C.** Leather can stretch.

○   ○   **D.** Shoes were made to fit either foot.

---

5. Jason and Josh were neighbors. They rode their bikes to school together every day. Josh got a new bike for his birthday. Jason wished he had a new bike, too. One day Josh left his bike in the yard. When he came back, it was gone.

Fact Inference

○   ○   **A.** Jason wanted a new bike.

○   ○   **B.** Josh and Jason rode to school together.

○   ○   **C.** Jason took Josh's bike.

○   ○   **D.** Josh and Jason were neighbors.

---

6. Jenna sat alone at the lunch table. It was her first day at the new school. Katie, a girl in Jenna's class, was sitting at another table with her friends. She noticed Jenna eating lunch by herself. Katie walked over to the table where Jenna was sitting.

Fact Inference

○   ○   **A.** Katie cared how Jenna felt.

○   ○   **B.** It was Jenna's first day at school.

○   ○   **C.** Katie walked to Jenna's table.

○   ○   **D.** Jenna was lonely.

Name_____   Date _____

Read the stories. Choose the sentence that best answers each question.

1. Ichabod Crane listened politely as the old man spoke. His voice was full of fear. He told Crane about a ghost. It was called the Headless Horseman. The ghost scared people who entered a place called Sleepy Hollow after dark. Crane laughed to himself as he listened to the story. That night Crane took a short cut through Sleepy Hollow. Before he knew it, the ghost was chasing him.

_____   Which of these sentences is probably true?

    A. The old man lived in Sleepy Hollow.
    B. Crane did not believe the man's story.
    C. Sleepy Hollow was far away.
    D. Crane liked to be scared.

---

2. The cowbird does not build a nest of its own. The mother cowbird lays her eggs in the nest of another bird. Then the cowbird leaves the eggs. She hopes the other bird will take care of her babies when they hatch.

_____   Which of these sentences is probably true?

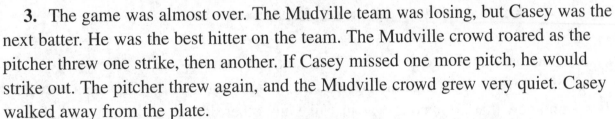

    A. The cowbird is lazy.
    B. Nests are hard to build.
    C. The cowbird is very caring.
    D. Baby cowbirds eat much food.

---

3. The game was almost over. The Mudville team was losing, but Casey was the next batter. He was the best hitter on the team. The Mudville crowd roared as the pitcher threw one strike, then another. If Casey missed one more pitch, he would strike out. The pitcher threw again, and the Mudville crowd grew very quiet. Casey walked away from the plate.

_____   Which of these sentences is probably true?

    A. Casey hit the ball over the fence.
    B. The crowd forgot to cheer.
    C. Casey's team won the game.
    D. On the last pitch, Casey struck out.

Name_____   Date _____

Read the stories. Choose the sentence that best answers each question.

1. Jim Smiley thought he was smarter than anyone else. Jim liked to be in contests, and he almost always won them. One day a new man arrived in town. This stranger offered to have a frog-jumping contest with Jim. Jim agreed and said he would find a good frog for the stranger. While Jim was gone, the stranger tied small weights to the legs of Jim's frog. Soon Jim returned with the stranger's frog.

_____ Which of these sentences is probably true?

   A. Jim's frog won the contest.
   B. The stranger's frog won the contest.
   C. Jim's frog jumped farther than it ever had.
   D. The frog tricked the stranger.

2. May Pierstorff took a strange trip in 1914. May's parents wanted her to visit her grandparents. They lived one hundred miles away. But a train ticket for May cost too much money. So her parents sent her by mail! It cost them 53 cents. May passed all the rules for being mailed. So May rode in the train mail car. She arrived safely.

_____ Which of these sentences is probably true?

   A. May's parents wanted to save money.
   B. May didn't want to visit her grandparents.
   C. May was lost in the mail.
   D. May tried to walk to her grandparents' house.

3. One day Ann heard her friend Tom talking. Tom was telling everybody how smart his dog was. Tom said his dog could do tricks and could even ride a bicycle. But Ann knew that Tom's dog was just like any other dog. So Ann just smiled as Tom went on talking.

_____ Which of these sentences is probably true?

   A. Ann didn't understand Tom's story.
   B. Tom wanted to make Ann mad at him.
   C. Ann didn't want to hurt Tom's feelings.
   D. Tom had two dogs and a cat.

Name_____ Date _____

Read the stories. Choose the sentence that best answers each question.

1. The day was sunny and hot. Ava stood happily at the side of the swimming pool. She thought about the clear, blue water. Then she jumped in. But as she began swimming, she started shaking, and her skin began to turn blue.

_____ Which of these sentences is probably true?

    A. The water was very hot.

    B. Ava forgot to wear her coat.

    C. The water was very cold.

    D. Ava didn't know how to swim.

---

2. When Louisa May Alcott was four, she had a birthday party. Many children were invited. Each child was supposed to get a small cake as a treat. Louisa handed out the cakes. She soon noticed that there were not enough cakes for everyone. One little girl was left in line, and there was only one cake left. Louisa wanted the cake for herself. But she smiled and gave the last cake to her friend.

_____ Which of these sentences is probably true?

    A. The last little girl wanted two cakes.

    B. Louisa was kind and sharing.

    C. The last little girl was not hungry.

    D. Louisa was not very friendly.

---

3. Nick sat trembling behind the couch as a storm roared outside. Lightning flashed and thunder rumbled. Each time the thunder rolled, Nick screamed loudly. Nick's dad tried to get the boy to come out, but Nick would not move.

_____ Which of these sentences is probably true?

    A. Storms made Nick's dad afraid.

    B. Nick liked to play hide and seek.

    C. Nick's dad made him feel better.

    D. Nick was afraid of thunder and lightning.

Name_____   Date _____

Read the stories. Choose the sentence that best answers each question.

1. At last the time came for Amy to give her report. She had to stand in front of the whole class and tell them about spiders. As she stood up, she dropped her report. The pages scattered all across the floor. Amy could feel everyone staring at her as she picked up the mess. Finally she reached the front of the room. She looked out at the class. Amy could feel her face turning red. She tried to speak, but no words would come out of her mouth.

_____   Which of these sentences is probably true?

    A. Amy was in the wrong class.

    B. The class was afraid of Amy.

    C. Talking in front of people was hard for Amy.

    D. Amy knew nothing about spiders.

2. It was a cold day, and Ali stared at the white snow that covered the sidewalk. He knew he had a lot of shoveling to do. He was supposed to clean off the whole sidewalk. Out in the street, Ali's friends were pulling their sleds. Ali knew they were going to have fun sledding down the hill. They called for him to come, but Ali just waved. As they walked away, Ali slowly started to shovel.

_____   Which of these sentences is probably true?

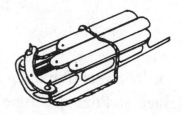

    A. Ali would rather work than play.

    B. The other children didn't like Ali.

    C. Ali loved to shovel snow.

    D. When Ali had a job to do, he did it.

3. If you are sick and you cough or sneeze on someone, that person could get sick, too. But it is not really a good idea to stop yourself from sneezing. If you do, you could pull a muscle in your face. You could also make your nose bleed.

_____   Which of these sentences is probably true?

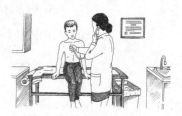

    A. Sneezing makes your nose bleed.

    B. Stopping a sneeze could be harmful.

    C. You can get over a cold by not sneezing.

    D. Sneezing is good exercise for your face.

Name_____   Date _____

Read the stories. Choose the sentence that best answers each question.

   1. Bob Hope was playing golf with a friend. His friend missed an easy shot. The angry friend threw his golf club into the tall grass. Bob secretly got the golf club back and started using it himself. Bob hit the ball a long way with his friend's club. The friend thought Bob's golf club was very good. He offered to buy it for fifty dollars. Bob sold the man the club he had just thrown away. Later Bob told his friend what had happened.

_____   Which of these sentences is probably true?
   A. Bob decided to keep his friend's golf club.
   B. Bob's friend felt silly for buying back his own club.
   C. Bob used the money to open a golf shop.
   D. Bob's friend never played golf again.

   2. Jo's mom was in the hospital. She had just had a new baby. Jo had seen the little thing with its wrinkled skin and its funny face. Jo was excited to have a new brother. But she was worried that her parents might not love her anymore.

_____   Which of these sentences is probably true?
   A. Jo's parents needed to tell her they could love two children.
   B. Jo did not like wrinkles or funny faces.
   C. Jo's mother was at home.
   D. Jo wanted a dog instead of a new baby brother.

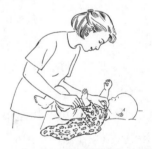

   3. The President was coming to visit the small town. Everyone was very excited. All the people worked hard to clean up their town. They mowed the grass and swept the sidewalks. They fixed up the old houses. They even painted the water tower.

_____   Which of these sentences is probably true?
   A. The President was moving to the town.
   B. The people were trying to fool the President.
   C. The President only liked big towns.
   D. The people wanted their town to look nice.

Name_____   Date _____

Read the stories. Choose the sentence that best answers each question.

1. Jim carefully lifted the eggs from their box. He handed two eggs to his mother. Then Jim measured a cup of milk, being careful not to spill any. He rubbed the cake pan with butter and watched as his mother poured in the batter. Then Jim and his mother cleaned up.

_____ Which of these sentences is probably true?

    A. Jim was a good helper.

    B. Jim's mother was a bad cook.

    C. Jim was hungry.

    D. Jim's mother was lazy.

---

2. Jan was always playing basketball. In fact, she almost never left the basketball court. Jan started practicing early every morning. As the sun went down, Jan was still bouncing the basketball.

_____ Which of these sentences is probably true?

    A. Jan slept at the basketball court.

    B. Tennis was very important to Jan.

    C. Jan wanted to be a great basketball player.

    D. The basketball was too big to bounce inside.

---

3. Nan was helping her uncle on the farm. He was loading the truck with hay for the cows. Nan's uncle threw a rope over the bales of hay. He told Nan to tie the rope carefully. But Nan only tied a loose knot. Then she hurried off to get a cool drink.

_____ Which of these sentences is probably true?

    A. All the cool drinks were already gone.

    B. The rope tightened itself.

    C. The knot came untied.

    D. The cool drink made Nan sick.

Name_____ Date _____

Read the stories. Mark whether each statement is an inference or a fact.

1. Have you ever caught fireflies on a warm summer night? Fireflies are interesting little insects. They make light with their bodies. But the light is not hot. Fireflies use their lights to send signals to other fireflies.

Fact Inference

○   ○   **A.** Fireflies come out in summer.

○   ○   **B.** The light of fireflies is not hot.

○   ○   **C.** Fireflies send signals with their lights.

○   ○   **D.** Fireflies can only send signals at night.

---

2. A long time ago, no one knew that dinosaurs had ever lived. But in 1822 an English woman found a large tooth. In a few years, other parts of these large reptiles known as dinosaurs were found.

Fact Inference

○   ○   **A.** Dinosaurs lived before 1822.

○   ○   **B.** Dinosaur bones were first found in England.

○   ○   **C.** A tooth was the first dinosaur bone found.

○   ○   **D.** Dinosaurs were reptiles.

---

3. William loved to go fishing. His grandfather had promised to take him on Saturday. That morning William packed a lunch and got his fishing pole ready. But about an hour before it was time to go, the phone rang. His grandfather said he was not feeling well and couldn't take William fishing. William was disappointed, but decided to make his grandfather a get-well card.

Fact Inference

○   ○   **A.** William was a caring person.

○   ○   **B.** William loved to go fishing.

○   ○   **C.** William loved his grandfather.

○   ○   **D.** William's grandfather was sick.

Name _____   Date _____

Read the stories. Mark whether each statement is an inference or a fact.

1. George Bidder was different from most boys his age. He was a whiz at math. When he was asked to work a math problem, he could do it in his head. Once he was told a 43-digit number backward. Right away he was able to switch it around in his head and say it forward in its correct order. He could even remember the number an hour later!

Fact Inference

○   ○   **A.** George worked math problems in his head.

○   ○   **B.** Math was George's favorite subject.

○   ○   **C.** George was a math whiz.

○   ○   **D.** People thought George was very smart.

---

2. The city was full of people on their way home. Buses, trucks, cars, and taxis crowded the streets. Mark was in a hurry to catch the bus. As he ran up to the bus stop, the bus roared away. Mark sat down on a nearby bench and frowned.

Fact Inference

○   ○   **A.** Mark ran to catch the bus.

○   ○   **B.** Mark was angry he missed the bus.

○   ○   **C.** The city streets were crowded.

○   ○   **D.** Mark was on his way home.

---

3. Sarah had not studied for the science test. Her friend Beth always did very well in science. Sarah sat beside Beth in class. When Mrs. Banes began passing out the science test, Sarah leaned over to Beth. "Write big so I can see," she whispered. Later, Mrs. Banes called the two girls to her desk.

Fact Inference

○   ○   **A.** Sarah had not studied.

○   ○   **B.** The girls were caught cheating.

○   ○   **C.** Beth did well in science.

○   ○   **D.** Sarah whispered to Beth.

Name _____   Date _____

Read the stories. Mark whether each statement is an inference or a fact.

1. It gets much hotter and much colder on the moon than here on Earth. At noon the temperature is four times higher on the moon than on Earth. For two weeks the moon stays dark all day long. This is called lunar night. At that time it is four times colder than on Earth.

Fact Inference

○   ○   **A.** The moon is coldest during lunar night.

○   ○   **B.** Lunar night lasts two weeks.

○   ○   **C.** The moon is hotter and colder than Earth.

○   ○   **D.** It is hottest on the moon at noon.

---

2. Miguel kicked the rocks in front of his feet. He had been excited about going to the rodeo. He wanted to see the cowboys do tricks. But now his mother wanted him to finish his farm work first. He slowly walked to the barn to water the horses. Then his brother's friend Ravon drove up in a truck. "How would you like a ride to the rodeo?" he asked.

Fact Inference

○   ○   **A.** The horses were thirsty.

○   ○   **B.** Miguel was excited about going to the rodeo.

○   ○   **C.** Ravon drove up in a truck.

○   ○   **D.** Miguel did not finish his work.

---

3. Mount St. Helens is a volcano in Washington. In 1980 it erupted for the first time in over one hundred years. Fire and melting rock poured out of the volcano. This caused rivers to flood. Four states were covered with ash. More than sixty people were killed.

Fact Inference

○   ○   **A.** Mount St. Helens erupted in 1980.

○   ○   **B.** The volcano did not erupt often.

○   ○   **C.** People lived near Mount St. Helens.

○   ○   **D.** Mount St. Helens is in Washington.

Name_____ Date _____

Read the stories. Mark whether each statement is an inference or a fact.

1. Mushrooms grow under piles of fallen leaves or on dead logs. People eat mushrooms in spaghetti or on pizza, but not all mushrooms are good to eat. Some mushrooms have poison in them. The poisonous ones are called toadstools.

Fact Inference

○ ○   **A.** Some mushrooms are poisonous.

○ ○   **B.** People eat mushrooms on pizza.

○ ○   **C.** Mushrooms grow on dead logs.

○ ○   **D.** People should not eat toadstools.

---

2. Maggie, Lauren, and Sandra were playing basketball. Lauren ran down the court, bouncing the ball. As she tried to shoot a basket, Maggie pushed the ball away. It bounced off the court and hit a parked car nearby. The ball smashed the car's back window. Maggie began running away. "Let's get out of here!" she yelled to her friends.

Fact Inference

○ ○   **A.** Maggie was afraid.

○ ○   **B.** The ball smashed the window.

○ ○   **C.** Maggie didn't plan to hit the car.

○ ○   **D.** Lauren and Sandra didn't follow Maggie.

---

3. What happens if the arm of a starfish gets cut off? It grows a new one! The body of a starfish is shaped like a star. Each point is an arm. A starfish has eyes and feet on its arms. Its eyes are little spots on the end of its arms. The feet of a starfish are like tiny tubes under each arm.

Fact Inference

○ ○   **A.** A starfish has feet.

○ ○   **B.** Starfish can grow new arms.

○ ○   **C.** A starfish can see.

○ ○   **D.** Starfish are shaped like stars.

Name_____   Date _____

Read the stories. Mark whether each statement is an inference or a fact.

1. Ted had been sick for a week. He had chicken pox. His teacher asked if anyone in the class could take Ted's homework to him. Dave had already had chicken pox, so he raised his hand. On his way to Ted's house, he bought some baseball cards for Ted.

Fact Inference

○   ○   **A.** Dave and Ted were friends.

○   ○   **B.** Ted had chicken pox.

○   ○   **C.** Dave raised his hand.

○   ○   **D.** Ted liked baseball cards.

---

2. People have used wheels for over five thousand years. They were probably first used in Middle Eastern countries. Chinese people learned to use the wheel about two thousand years later. Indians in North and South America did not use wheels for work at that time. But they did put wheels on their toys.

Fact Inference

○   ○   **A.** Some Native American toys had wheels.

○   ○   **B.** People in China used wheels to do work.

○   ○   **C.** China is not in the Middle East.

○   ○   **D.** Wheels have been used for a long time.

---

3. "Come right home after school," Ann's mom told her. "I will," said Ann. She waved goodbye and rode off on her bike to school. On her way home, Ann saw some of her friends at the park. They were riding their bikes through a mud puddle. It looked like fun. Ann decided to join them.

Fact Inference

○   ○   **A.** Ann rode her bike to school.

○   ○   **B.** Ann was late getting home.

○   ○   **C.** Ann's friends were at the park.

○   ○   **D.** Ann did not obey her mother.

Name _____   Date _____

Read the stories. Mark whether each statement is an inference or a fact.

1. The Vikings were probably first to find North America. Ruins of Viking houses have been found in Newfoundland. Their houses were built around A.D. 1000. English fishers probably didn't reach that area until 1481. Columbus thought he was the first one to find the New World in 1492.

Fact Inference

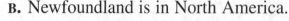
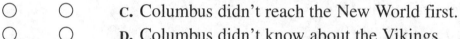

○   ○   **A.** Vikings built houses about A.D. 1000.
○   ○   **B.** Newfoundland is in North America.
○   ○   **C.** Columbus didn't reach the New World first.
○   ○   **D.** Columbus didn't know about the Vikings.

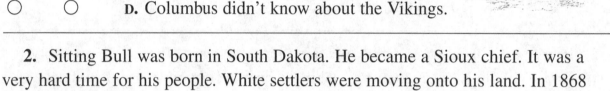

2. Sitting Bull was born in South Dakota. He became a Sioux chief. It was a very hard time for his people. White settlers were moving onto his land. In 1868 the United States asked the Sioux and Cheyenne chiefs to sign a peace treaty. Many chiefs signed the treaty and lived on the reservation. But Sitting Bull did not. He wanted to live the old way.

Fact Inference

○   ○   **A.** Sitting Bull was a Sioux chief.
○   ○   **B.** Sitting Bull did not like the white settlers.
○   ○   **C.** Sitting Bull did not sign the treaty.
○   ○   **D.** Sitting Bull did not want to change.

3. When we think of windmills, we often think of Holland. The people there used windmills to take water off their land. That way they had more land for farming. Now windmills are used to make electricity.

Fact Inference

○   ○   **A.** There is not enough farmland in Holland.
○   ○   **B.** Farmland must be fairly dry.
○   ○   **C.** Holland has many windmills.
○   ○   **D.** Now windmills make electricity.

COMPREHENSION: GRADE 4
ANSWER KEY

Unit I: Facts

Assessment, p. 11-12
1. D
2. D
3. A
4. C
5. B
6. C
7. D
8. A
9. D
10. B

Lesson 1, pp. 13-14
1. B
2. B
3. A
4. C
5. D
6. B
7. C
8. D
9. A
10. D

Lesson 2, pp. 15-16
1. A
2. A
3. C
4. D
5. D
6. A
7. D
8. C
9. B
10. D

Lesson 3, pp. 17-18
1. B
2. A
3. C
4. B
5. C
6. B
7. C
8. A
9. D
10. D

Lesson 4, pp. 19-20
1. C
2. D
3. C
4. B
5. D
6. A
7. D
8. D
9. C
10. B

Lesson 5, pp. 21-22
1. D
2. B
3. A
4. D
5. C
6. B
7. A
8. D

9. C
10. B

Lesson 6, pp. 23-24
1. B
2. B
3. A
4. D
5. B
6. C
7. D
8. C
9. D
10. B

Unit II: Sequence

Assessment, pp. 25-26
1. 1, 3, 2
2. A
3. A
4. C
5. B

Lesson 1, p. 28
1. 2, 1, 3
2. C
3. A
4. B
5. C

Lesson 2, p. 30
1. 3, 2, 1
2. A
3. A
4. C
5. A

Lesson 3, p. 32
1. 2, 3, 1
2. A
3. C
4. B
5. C

Lesson 4, p. 34
1. 2, 1, 3
2. C
3. A
4. B
5. A

Lesson 5, p. 36
1. 3, 2, 1
2. C
3. A
4. B
5. A

Lesson 6, p. 38
1. 3, 1, 2
2. C
3. A
4. B
5. A

Unit III: Context

Assessment, pp. 39-40
1. A
2. B
3. C
4. B

5. A
6. B
7. A
8. D
9. B
10. A
11. C
12. C

Lesson 1, p. 41
1. C
2. D
3. B
4. C
5. C
6. B
7. A
8. C

Lesson 2, p. 42
1. B
2. D
3. A
4. C
5. D
6. B
7. D
8. A

Lesson 3, p. 43
1. D
2. A
3. A
4. C
5. C
6. A
7. B
8. D

Lesson 4, p. 44
1. C
2. B
3. C
4. A
5. B
6. C
7. A
8. B

Lesson 5, p. 45
1. C
2. B
3. A
4. B
5. A
6. B
7. C
8. D

Lesson 6, p. 46
1. B
2. A
3. B
4. D
5. A
6. C
7. A
8. D

Lesson 7, p. 47
1. C
2. A
3. B
4. D

Lesson 8, p. 48
1. C
2. D
3. B
4. C

Lesson 9, p. 49
1. C
2. B
3. D
4. A

Lesson 10, p. 50
1. C
2. D
3. C
4. B

Lesson 11, p. 51
1. D
2. B
3. A
4. C

Lesson 12, p. 52
1. B
2. D
3. C
4. C

Unit IV: Main Idea

Assessment, pp. 53-54
1. C
2. B
3. C
4. A
5. B
6. C

Lesson 1, p. 55
1. A
2. C
3. B

Lesson 2, p. 56
1. B
2. C
3. B

Lesson 3, p. 57
1. C
2. B
3. B

Lesson 4, p. 58
1. C
2. C
3. A

Lesson 5, p. 59
1. B
2. C
3. A

Lesson 6, p. 60
1. A
2. A
3. B

Lesson 7, p. 61
1. A
2. A
3. A

Lesson 8, p. 62
1. A
2. B
3. A

Lesson 9, p. 63
1. B
2. C
3. D

Lesson 10, p. 64
1. C
2. A
3. D

Lesson 11, p. 65
1. A
2. C
3. C

Lesson 12, p. 66
1. C
2. A
3. B

Unit V: Conclusion
Assessment, pp. 67-68
1. C
2. B
3. C
4. A
5. B
6. D

Lesson 1, p. 69
1. B
2. C
3. A

Lesson 2, p. 70
1. C
2. B
3. D

Lesson 3, p. 71
1. A
2. A
3. B

Lesson 4, p. 72
1. B
2. B
3. C

Lesson 5, p. 73
1. B
2. C
3. A

Lesson 6, p. 74
1. C
2. D
3. B

Lesson 7, p. 75
1. D
2. C
3. A

Lesson 8, p. 76
1. A
2. D
3. C

Lesson 9, p. 77
1. C
2. B
3. D

Lesson 10, p. 78
1. A
2. B
3. D

Lesson 11, p. 79
1. B
2. D
3. A

Lesson 12, p. 80
1. B
2. D
3. A

Unit VI: Inference
Assessment, pp. 81-82
1. C
2. B
3. B
4. A. F
   B. I
   C. I
   D. F
5. A. F
   B. F
   C. I
   D. F
6. A. I
   B. F
   C. F
   D. I

Lesson 1, p. 83
1. B
2. A
3. D

Lesson 2, p. 84
1. B
2. A
3. C

Lesson 3, p. 85
1. C
2. B
3. D

Lesson 4, p. 86
1. C
2. D
3. B

Lesson 5, p. 87
1. B
2. A
3. D

Lesson 6, p. 88
1. A
2. C
3. C

Lesson 7, p. 89
1. A. I
   B. F
   C. F
   D. I
2. A. I
   B. I
   C. F
   D. F
3. A. I
   B. F
   C. I
   D. F

Lesson 8, p. 90
1. A. F
   B. I
   C. F
   D. I
2. A. F
   B. I
   C. F
   D. I
3. A. F
   B. I
   C. F
   D. F

Lesson 9, p. 91
1. A. I
   B. F
   C. F
   D. I
2. A. I
   B. F
   C. F
   D. I
3. A. F
   B. I
   C. I
   D. F

Lesson 10, p. 92
1. A. F
   B. F
   C. F
   D. I
2. A. I
   B. F
   C. I
   D. I
3. A. F
   B. F
   C. I
   D. F

Lesson 11, p. 93
1. A. I
   B. F
   C. F
   D. I
2. A. F
   B. I
   C. I
   D. F
3. A. F
   B. I
   C. F
   D. I

Lesson 12, p. 94
1. A. F
   B. I
   C. I
   D. I
2. A. F
   B. I
   C. F
   D. I
3. A. I
   B. I
   C. I
   D. F